OPTIMIZING PEOPLE

Reuven Bar-On, Ph.D.
&
Rich Handley, DBA

Published by Pro-Philes Press
1107 Gruene Road
New Braunfels, Texas 78130

Library of Congress Catalog Number 98-68109

Library of Congress Cataloging-In-Publication Data on file with the publisher.

CONTENTS

Foreword

Why this book was written and what it's about

Optimizing People was originally designed as a brief remedial guide to be used with the world's first test of emotional and social intelligence called the EQ-i (Bar-On, 1997). Its original purpose was to help EQ-i users better understand their results and to offer simple straightforward suggestions aimed at improving those emotional and social skills in need of improvement. Based on the way this book has developed, it has not only accomplished its original aim but has gone far beyond it. We now recommend that this book be used as a comprehensive handbook of emotional and social intelligence to assist EQ-i users as well as the general reader to better understand the factors involved and how to improve them.

This is not another *EQ book,* but rather one co-authored by the person who coined the term "EQ" in 1985 and who published the first test of emotional and social intelligence (Bar-On, 1997) based on the most comprehensive model of this concept.

Optimizing People is the product of an exciting joint venture. Dr. Bar-On brought to this venture the concept and measure of emotional and social intelligence, and Dr. Handley has creatively applied it to the corporate world creating a new science. This book is not about another theory that is hard to understand, impossible to prove, or difficult to use, but it is about an operational concept that has been scientifically developed, tested, and successfully applied in the real world. It has not only proven itself as a powerful and valuable concept in the workplace, but has been successfully applied in educational, marital, medical, and mental health settings as will be seen in the introductory chapter. Both authors bring years of professional experience and a pioneering spirit to this endeavor. It is a pleasure to share this knowledge and exciting to know that the reader will be exposed to an opportunity for a valuable learning experience.

This book is designed to walk the reader through a basic understanding of what emotional and social intelligence is, why it is important for the individual and for organizations, and how to improve it and apply it in the workplace. Broadly speaking, this concept addresses the emotional, personal, social, and survival dimensions of intelligence, which are often more important for daily functioning than the more cognitive or mental aspects of intelligence. This part of intelligence is concerned with understanding oneself and others, relating to people, and adapting to and coping with the immediate surroundings, which increases one's ability to be more successful in dealing with daily demands. Emotional and social intelligence is tactical (immediate functioning), while cognitive intelligence is strategic (long-term capacity). Emotional and social intelligence helps to predict success because it reflects how a person applies knowledge of a more personal and interpersonal nature to the immediate situation. In a way, this type of intelligence can be thought of as "common sense" (or "street smarts") and one's ability to get along in the world. A more precise definition is presented in the beginning of the introductory chapter.

The Bar-On model and measure of emotional and social intelligence evolved out of Dr. Bar-On's work as a clinical psychologist over a period of nearly two decades. As a result of his early clinical experience, he began to ask, *Why do some people succeed in possessing better emotional health than others?* This question then expanded into, *Why are some individuals more able to succeed in life than others?* These questions commanded a thorough study of factors (emotional, personal, and social abilities and skills) thought to determine general success, in addition to success in possessing and maintaining positive emotional health. It soon became clear that the key determinant predicting success is not always, only, or even (in some cases) cognitive intelligence — many cognitively intelligent people flounder in life, while many emotionally and socially intelligent individuals succeed and prosper.

This concept has met with a great deal of popularity by professional and lay people alike. Part of this popularity most likely stems from the fact that it is easy to understand and, unlike cognitive intelligence, can be improved. We feel that it offers *hope* to many people who can actively do something to make themselves more effective, efficient, and successful in life.

Improving emotional and social skills increases one's ability to become more efficient and successful in the workplace, and more efficient and successful employees will, in turn, increase the overall productivity of their organization as a whole based on our findings.

This book is recommended for use in the corporate setting as a reference source for understanding and improving emotional and social skills relevant to the workplace. Potential users include psychologists, vocational counselors, human resources professionals, organizational development consultants, and managers.

So, what is this book actually about, what is our bottom line, and why is it important for you to read it?

- This book is about improving organizational performance, about making organizations more effective and productive. It's neither rocket science nor voodoo. It's based on many years of sophisticated empirical research, but is definitely very straightforward, comprehensible, and immediately applicable. Making organizations more effective and productive is done by focusing on the greatest source of leverage available today for organizations seeking to make the leap to the true high-performance frontier. This source of leverage and key to success is PEOPLE...your employees. Being able to attract, promote, and hold on to this most valuable asset (human capital) is the single biggest predictor of corporate excellence among the world's most admired companies (Fortune Magazine, October 27, 1997). The last corporate secret is to know who you are looking for and how to "pick" those with the right stuff, and the key to this secret is to know what exactly is the right stuff and how to measure it.
- This book is about the single biggest factor that leverages the success

of people, which is emotional and social intelligence (the people skills that routinely characterize those with the right stuff).

- This book is about how to use emotional and social intelligence in an intelligent way to boost the skills that equate to success in the current workforce.
- This book is about applying EQ to first know exactly what you're looking for, then how to use it to find and hire those with the kind of talent that companies will bet their lives on.
- This book is about how to tap EQ with the EQ-i in order to plan on-target investments in human development.
- This book is about how to scientifically apply emotional and social intelligence in the workplace to develop the kind of managerial skills that are required in the era of the knowledge worker.
- In summary, this book is about human capital profiling based on applying the emotional-social-behavioral audit to examine organizational aerodynamics and sculpt corporate culture to decrease drag and increase top-end performance and efficiency. Finally, for organizations who use human capital profiling, it helps them mean it when they say that "people are our most important asset."

This is the first edition of *Optimizing People*, and we welcome and encourage your feedback, which will be molded into future editions of this book together with our research findings and those of others in this field. Correspondence with the authors can be sent to our web site (**www.pro-philes.com**).

Authors' Preface

The importance of applying emotional and social intelligence in the workplace

In applied psychology, it is important to make concepts tangible by defining them as clearly as possible. These "operational" concepts then need to be examined so that they can be applied in the real world. This is exactly the approach that was adopted in developing the Bar-On conceptual model of emotional and social intelligence, which one of the co-authors has been systematically developing since 1980. The Emotional Quotient Inventory (EQ-i) was constructed primarily to examine and measure that model, and the findings that it has generated over the years have continued to refine the concept. In the last couple of years, we have been busy exposing psychologists, employment counselors, human resources consultants, organizational development professionals, and senior executives to this model and measure, helping them to integrate it into their repertoire. We have been helping professionals in various organizational settings to revise their recruitment and selection procedures as well as to develop training strategies for improving emotional and social skills in the workplace. The importance of applying this approach in the workplace is discussed below.

Leveraging Corporate Performance through Human Capital Profiling

Thomas Stewart, of *Fortune Magazine* and author of *Intellectual Capital* (Stewart, 1997), suggests that corporate America is now built on *intellectual capital* rather than bricks and mortar, and he feels that this is changing everything. Indeed, we have seen the transition to the *era of the knowledge worker* focus on what's between the workers' ears as the most valuable asset of the organization, and this asset goes home with them every day. In the era of intellectual capital, these human skills (such as assertiveness, problem solving, flexibility, judgment, creativity, and so forth) will be the most valuable. Alfred Sloan, the first modern CEO, who became chief of GM in 1920 when the auto-maker was struggling against Ford Motor Company, said it best: "Take my assets but leave me my organization, and in five years I'll have it all back." According to an article that appeared in *Fortune Magazine* on September 18, 1995, over 39 percent of the US workforce is made up of knowledge workers, and 43 percent of the net employment growth from 1990 to 1995 was in *high-knowledge industries* (industries in which over 40 percent of the workers are knowledge workers).

Managing in the era of the knowledge worker requires a fundamental shift or change in the way companies manage their assets. Speaking of change, former British Prime Minister Harold Wilson once noted, "He who rejects change is the architect of decay, and the only human institution which rejects progress is the cemetery." The change that we must grasp is that knowledge workers own the tools of production (which is their knowledge), and the company merely borrows it. When discussing the "economic importance of community," Ed McCracken, CEO of Silicon Graphics, was quoted as saying (*Inc. Magazine,* November 1996):

In an information-age company, people are your greatest resource. And that resource goes home every night to the community, and they either will or will not come back the next morning. The most enlightened companies view all their employees as freelancers who are independent entrepreneurs. They just happen to be inside your boundaries and on your payroll, but in fact they can choose to live and work anywhere. So the quality and vitality of the community matters a great deal — it affects employees' ideas, what they bring to the job, and their staying power with the company.

The future of corporate structure requires a change from the hierarchical command-and-control management structure. Paul Saffo, of Institute for the Future, a trend forecasting organization, foresees the corporate management model to be based on biological models inspired more by behavior of *organisms and communities* (Saffo, 1996). His prediction is for the structure to be *web-like* with the rigid hierarchies disappearing in favor of *rich, flexible, and constantly changing relationship webs*. This model places less importance on power by title and more on power based upon position in the web. The idea is much like the internet — those occupying particularly rich nodes in the network will wield enormous influence, regardless of title. Saffo predicts that those capable of *adapting* most quickly to changing environments and conditions will do the best. The irony of this is that in an era in which many question the loyalty of the company towards the employee due to corporate downsizing, rightsizing, restructuring, and change in benefits, most companies will be more dependent than ever on the knowledge of their employees. Peter Drucker, who coined the term *knowledge worker*, feels that in the knowledge society, the most probable assumption for organizations — and certainly the assumption on which they have to conduct their affairs — is that they need knowledge workers, far more than knowledge workers need them (Drucker, 1995). The *Wall Street Journal* (September 3, 1997) indicates that the top priority of a CEO is to enhance intellectual capital by better managing human relationships. The article goes on to say that this, however, is a "tall order in an era when loyalty has been blunted by corporate downsizing but nevertheless is important because companies now depend heavily on employees for creative insights that only the enthusiastic can offer." This has also had an effect on the knowledge workers themselves, many in a sense becoming free agents. In the annual Information Technology Job Satisfaction Survey of 503 respondents published in *Computerworld* (May 26, 1997), it was revealed that 17 percent of senior IS executives, 30 percent of the IS middle managers and 33 percent of the IS professionals indicated that they were "always" seeking new job opportunities. Another interesting point that was revealed is that 39 percent of the senior IS executives and 60 percent of the

IS managers and professionals indicated that they didn't feel that they were working to their fullest potential. So the bottom line is that companies will have to work to maintain their intellectual capital, most specifically finding and keeping those specific skill sets that equate to the reason customers do business with them versus someone else. Michael Milken, the former junk bond king, noted in *Business Week* (August 4, 1997) that the human capital market (a $100 billion industry according to him) is the biggest opportunity around; more specifically, this appears to be in the area of consulting related to human capital assets.

That said, where do we begin? We begin in the same place where companies take stock of their corporate fiscal position — the audit, more specifically, *the human capital audit*. The trick is to operationalize the *soft stuff* and make it hard so that we can begin to manage from a value-added human capital structure. This means identifying the skill sets that provide a high rate of return and a positive return on training investment, which truly are corporate assets and are a source of competitive advantage. *Human capital profiling* is the way to operationalize the soft stuff, which has traditionally been harder for managers to manage than fiscal assets.

The idea of conducting a human capital audit is to profile the corporate position, providing a behavioral health and emotional-social balance sheet so that we can conduct a strategic assessment of our human capital position: strengths, weaknesses, opportunities, and threats. The goal of addressing the behavioral health issues is to decrease risk factors that represent organizational drag and increase protective factors to minimize drag effect. For example, a *behavioral health audit* would attempt to first ascertain what percent of the workforce struggles at any given time with depression, substance abuse, or stress management issues. The next step would then be to calculate what that costs the organization and how it impacts the bottom line.

Conducting an *emotional-social audit*, or more specifically an *emotional and social intelligence audit*, allows the company to profile what emotional and social skill sets are associated with high performance. This helps in the area of recruitment and selection on the one hand, and in retention, training, and team development on the other. First, by profiling what emotional and social skill sets are associated with high performance in various corporate positions (like sales, marketing, management, and so forth), the company gains leverage in finding and hiring people with the "right stuff." Secondly, an emotional-social audit helps the company find and *enhance* those skill sets that truly constitute a corporate asset that can give the company the needed competitive advantage. This is vital for gaining high leverage for on-target companies investing in human capital development. This twofold approach (hiring people with emotional and social skill sets that match well with the skills of high performers presently in those jobs, and then training them further in these specific areas) has a compound leverage effect. Additionally, since their skills match well with the profile of the high performers and thus increase their likelihood for success, this approach will aid in retaining employees with the right stuff.

Sadly enough however, these issues are often neglected until something blows up. This creates problematic situations that lurk under the radar of many companies and managers, and constitutes what is called "human capital drag" that costs and costs and costs! In aeronautics, "profile drag" is created by the profile of the object as air flows over it. The idea from the aeronautical world is that drag decreases performance requiring increased thrust to overcome it, thus causing the expenditure of more energy or resources to maintain performance equal to what we could have achieved with less energy expenditure simply by decreasing drag. The constant quest in aeronautics has been to *reduce* drag to improve performance and *improve* efficiency. In today's downsized corporate environment, any needless expenditure of resources makes a big difference. Companies can't be competitive in the global market operating with inefficient "human capital drag" profiles. Operating with significant drag due to behavioral health problems and/or emotional and social skill deficits is like a huge 747 with the landing gear and flaps down, continuing to apply throttle, in an effort to keep up with a supersonic Concord. Yet, many companies operate with this type of human capital aerodynamic profile, trying to become the sleek, efficient, agile, high-performance craft that it will take to maintain superiority in the global corporate environment of the future. The future requires "fast" companies, companies with the high-performance characteristics that allow them to make steep turns to avoid danger, or to quickly respond to rapid market changes, or to kick in the afterburner and lose the competition. Unfortunately, many companies today are like lumbering blimps, slowly maneuvering and responding, with tremendous profile drag; they simply will not survive. It's startling to realize how some companies can exhibit a high degree of sophisticated resource management and fiscal acumen on the one hand, but don't have a clue as to the amount of organizational emotional-social-behavioral drag they are operating with on the other hand. Once these factors can be put into a dollar cost, they seem to take on a whole new perspective to management. These issues probably constitute the biggest performance drag experienced by many organizations today. The question management must ask is: "What is our threshold for pain?" And more specifically on the behavioral side: "Can we tolerate a slow bleed to the tune of $4 million a year due to the cost of stress-related disorders (not only in treatment costs but in lost productivity and job turnover)?" Or on the emotional-social skill side: "Can we afford two hundred mismatches yearly in new hires who didn't have the 'right stuff' and didn't make it, with a lost training cost of $20,000 each?" "What amount of energy will we have to continue to expend to overcome this drag and maintain the performance parameters we want?" "How agile can we be in the high angle of attack and high-performance future with this type of drag?" These are tough questions, and many companies today seem to be asleep at the wheel on this issue.

The Behavioral Health Audit (BQ)

As was previously stated, the purpose of doing a behavioral health audit in an organization is to decrease risk factors and increase protective factors. This is carried out by what we call *organizational behavioral health profiling* coupled with *organization-specific prevention prescriptions,* versus generic prevention or no prevention. Profiling is similar to evaluating the aerodynamics of an aircraft through wind tunnel testing. It allows us to evaluate efficiency and drag factors and make the appropriate modifications to improve performance. Some organizations seem to operate in this area according to the old maxim, "If it ain't broke...don't fix it" or "Who cares about aerodynamics or efficiency, just pour the throttle to it" (which means spend more resources). "If we can't get the performance we want this way, let's just strap a bigger engine on" (which means throw more money at the problem), or worse yet, the way to improve the performance of your people is to turn up the heat. The fault in this logic is that many organizations have hit the performance wall that this type of human capital management creates, and these companies will never be able to make the jump to warp speed. Some managers seem to operate in this regard out of fear: "I'm afraid to conduct a behavioral health audit for fear of what I might find — so, I'll deal with it when I have to." This is like flying an aircraft or driving a car without an oil pressure indicator, or with it but refusing to look at it. Continuing this line of logic in an effort to see it the way they see it, it would be preferable to rip the oil pressure indicator out of the dash in order not to be bothered by receiving early warnings of potential trouble and by having to take the necessary corrective action. It appears that they would rather be surprised! Either way, we are responsible to deal with the end result — so, we have to decide if we want to be forewarned or not.

What are some of the likely targets for the behavioral health audit? They are numerous, but those that represent a *high return* are: absenteeism, smoking, alcohol abuse, physical fitness, weight management, life event stressors, anxiety and depression, workplace violence, and relationship difficulties with significant others. Chrysler Corporation reported a 6 percent absenteeism rate for 1997, up from 5.2 percent in 1996, costing the automaker $72 million. (*Wall Street Journal*, August 26, 1997). Stress alone can have a devastating effect on workforce effectiveness. The worksite wellness movement has continued to demonstrate the payoff for organizational-specific interventions. For example, high levels of involvement in corporate fitness programs have been correlated with lower levels of absenteeism, reduced medical claims, higher productivity, decreased turnover, improved decision-making, and higher morale. Personal problems cost companies approximately $2 billion dollars annually according to the International Foundation of Employee Benefit Plans. This has prompted many employers to look at employee assistance programs (EAPs) to help address this issue of helping employees with personal and work-related problems while managing benefit costs. According to the US Department of Labor, EAPs save employers up to $16 for every dollar invested. Worker absenteeism fell 16 percent in 1996 based on the 1997 survey of 451 employers at the Commerce Clearing House in Chicago; this was noted as the first decline since 1992. Speculation as to the reason for this ranged from fear of punishment and a strong work ethic to corporate attempts to curb absenteeism by helping employees with personal problems (*Wall Street Journal*, August 26, 1997). Depression affects one in five Americans. Researchers at MIT and Paul Greenberg at Analysis Group Economics in Cambridge, Massachusetts, put the cost of depression at $44 billion yearly, with $24 billion of that in absenteeism and lost productivity (*Fortune*, October 13, 1997). In a recent behavioral health audit that one of the authors conducted on a large nationwide mobile sales force involving over four hundred personnel, it was noted that personnel who were involved in aerobic activity three or more times weekly (36 percent) scored highest on total well-being, were more relaxed, scored higher on stress management, were less depressed, and exhibited reduced type A behavior (associated with a lower risk of heart attack). To no surprise, those who were involved in aerobic exercise at least one to two days a week (31 percent) scored next highest in these areas, and those who did no exercise (33 percent) scored the worst. Incidentally, those who exercised the most were also noted to be the most productive salespeople. Many may question this link to corporate performance, but again back to the aircraft analogy: higher sales performance came from those "aircraft" (salespeople) that were optimally maintained (those who exercised three or more times weekly). Reduced performance came from those who were less than optimally *maintained*. Which type of aircraft would you trust? Continuing with the aircraft analogy, optimal maintenance indeed appears to ensure peak performance. The ancient Greeks' idea of the importance of balance between body, mind, and soul is recalled when reviewing the results of these studies. To be out of balance in one or more of these areas creates drag that hampers our ability to be a "top gun." Perhaps one of the greater human tragedies is people living beneath their true capability. Simply because they have been their so long, these people believe this is the best they can do, or worse, they have been told or led to believe this is all they can hope for. It is obvious that corporations will have to act or get acted upon. Today's corporate environment is a come-as-you-are type scenario. The victors will be those who can successfully wage continuous operations, over a widely dispersed, highly fluid global ecosystem exploiting a combination of tool systems and human systems. This new corporate environment has produced a new generation of business leaders and has revolutionized the way we will have to do business. Geoffrey James, author of *Business Wisdom of the Electronic Elite* (1996), indicates that the *electronic elite* (companies such as Microsoft, COMPAQ, Hewlett-Packard, and so forth) have been successful in navigating this new frontier because of the changes to their corporate cultures. Basically, the managers of these companies have transitioned from the traditional hierarchies and corporate *warfare* tactics of the Industrial Revolution to the new practices of the Digital Revolution and the Information Age. The basic shift is treating business as an *ecosystem* (not as a *battlefield*) from treating the corporations as well-oiled machines that are run, not led, using command-and-control tactics and treating employees as cogs that could be replaced when necessary to improve the machine's performance. This strategy tended to dehumanize people, treating the system itself as more important than the people who comprise the system. The shift is towards viewing the company as a *community*, the role of management being to serve rather than control, treating employees as peers, or co-owners, versus children. This approach focuses on motivation by inspiration rather than through fear and intimidation, embracing change as a source of growth not pain. James outlines thirty-four strategies that characterize this new era that are worthy of a good read. For the doubters, this new corporate culture is not just a fad but will be around for a long time to come. To evidence that fact, James notes that other businesses are copying that culture, noting particularly that the Asian companies have started imitating these *electronic elite* because of their belief in doing what works, as the Japanese did when they picked up on Edwards Deming and the TQM concept.

Doug Englebart, the visionary icon of the computer revolution (and inventor of the mouse, multiple windows on computer screens, groupware, hypertext, and so forth), advocates the vision of people (*human systems*) using technology (*tool systems*) to improve the *collective IQ* of organizations. His vision calls for the co-evolution of human systems with tool systems for truly high-performing organizations. Obviously, the co-evolution has largely been one-sided, with the evolution skewed more towards technology. In tomorrow's digital frontier, it will be those organizations who masterfully can exploit the digital power of computers to augment human intellect that will be the *superpowers* of the global corporate future. Englebart believes that the formula for organizational change is dependent upon people using technology to improve the collective IQ of their companies, building collaborative communities of knowledge workers, and using the concurrent development, integration, and application of knowledge capabilities. The bottom line is using *human* and *technical* systems to enhance an organization's improvement processes (getting better at getting better) and overall performance. His model emphasizes the obvious, that it's time for companies to start addressing building high-performance human systems with the same gusto they've demonstrated in obtaining high-performance *tool systems*.

Finally, the greater logic behind this shift in the way we view the workplace makes sense because people spend the greatest part of their waking hours in the workplace. Harvard economist Juliet Schor indicates that Americans work an average of 164 more hours a year than they did in 1970, before computers were so common in the workplace. The implication is that since burnout can be a serious problem in the workplace, the workplace should be enjoyable, promoting a balance between family and personal life, and work life. It is interesting to witness the rankings found in several major business magazines listing the top companies in this category. This approach, as evidenced by the *electronic elite*, places value on employees, treating them as members of the community, offering education, training, and personal development opportunities that enhance their employee's careers. The return on this investment is that the companies get more skilled and loyal employees who are committed to the community's goals, being a stakeholder and co-owner, versus a *cog*.

The Emotional and Social Audit (EQ)

In addition to the behavioral health issues described above, emotional and social issues are also taken into account in the human capital audit. Profiling *emotional and social* skill sets aids in the recruitment, selection, and retention of employees; it is also helpful in career development and training, team building, and in organizational restructuring.

Recruiting, selecting and retaining employees:

According to a survey of 1,846 small and midsize US and Canadian businesses (*Inc. Magazine*, March 1997), the biggest management challenge is finding and training new employees. In another survey of 838 company owners (*Inc. Magazine*, July 1996), it was felt it was harder than it was five years ago to find the right employees. In the same sources, manufacturers complained of high turnover costs and noted that recruiting fees, training costs, and lost productivity were big expenses. Perhaps this has fostered another current trend: *the modern job interview*. These interviews range from the think fast brainteasers to being creative with a paper bag to behavioral simulation...all in the quest of finding people with the "right stuff." The problem is: What is the right stuff, whose right stuff is it, how do you know it's the right stuff, and how do you measure it? Robert Sternberg of Yale concludes (1996) that common sense or *tacit knowledge* is a better predictor of job performance than IQ. One must wonder how successful these current interview practices are in addressing these "right stuff" questions and finding employees with this type of common sense. A far better method would be to profile and differentiate emotional and social intelligence skill sets (common sense and tactical street smarts). This is a more accurate way of determining if there really are differences between the high performer and the average worker, and what exactly these differences are if indeed they exist. Once this can be determined, a benchmark is created to more accurately evaluate potential applicants who may possess the "right stuff" (instead of just IQ or degrees held); this then avoids much of the current *voodoo* being practiced in this area and makes recruitment and selection much more scientific. Additionally, this is a way to profile corporate culture by looking at the overall corporate EQ profile. The different occupational and professional groups as well as the various departments in the organization can also be profiled. Screening potential employees against these "right stuff" emotional and social skill profiles not only provides a way to evaluate the degree of fit between the candidates and the specific job for which they are being considered, but the degree of fit with the corporate culture as a whole. For example, in a fast-paced and constantly changing corporate culture, individuals low in flexibility and stress tolerance may not be suitable. The profiling of emotional and social skills also allows for the targeting of what specific skill sets workers need to move along career paths and make the transition from what they know now, to what they will need to know in the future. Thus, this type of profiling provides vital information for on-target investment in employee development, another potent tool that aids in employee retention. It also provides a basic set of specific job requisite skills (the "right stuff") that go a long way in ensuring the greatest chance for success of new employees within their respective career fields. This again can significantly aid employee development and retention. Finally, personal coaching or mentoring employees based on the continued development of these emotional and social skills, particularly for those in executive leadership positions, is powerful method to improve corporate culture and retention. Ensuring top-down skill set development is critical. It will do little good to bring in new hires with suitable skills only to expose them to an organizational EQ virus from an infected organizational culture or leadership structure. It is very interesting to note that while many companies devote significant energy and resources towards employee recruitment, a corporate position in charge of employee retention is non-existent. Perhaps the shift should be towards ombudsmen or mentors who are personally responsible for sponsoring new employees ensuring their assimilation within the corporate culture and facilitating their continual development.

Career development and training of employees:

In assessing the impact of spending money for corporate training and employee development, one of our faulty models has been that learning correlates with training and the expenditure of resources for this purpose. Wrong! First, how do we know what skills are needed to move along career paths, to close the gap between those skills which personnel currently possess and those they need to possess? Second, how much do we spend on training, and how much of that really hits the mark? Again, we seem to follow the analogy of "spend it, and they will learn" and "since we spent it, it's bound to hit the mark." Throughout the 1990s, experts have advocated a broad range of *human capital strategies* to boost productivity and position US workers to compete in the global economy (*Business Week*, September 15, 1997). Previously, worries about controlling costs scared employers away from investing in long-term training and education programs for their workforce; but, with today's profits hitting forty-year highs, there is beginning to be a shift towards devoting more resources to workforce education. An additional factor that is influencing this is that labor markets are tightening, and companies are having to invest more in the development of their workforce. The Economic Policy Institute indicates that nearly a third of all workers are in lower-skilled jobs, paying less than $15,000 annually. This has produced an incentive for a tidal wave of applicants looking for well-paying jobs that don't require a college degree (surprisingly, a category that includes three quarters of all jobs according to the previous source). The hitch, of course, is that the employers must train them. When we profile emotional and social skill sets, it gives us a handy perspective of what skills the workforce will likely need to perform certain tasks, based upon the traits associated with those who are currently successful in those roles. Second, it helps us find and enhance skill sets that truly constitute corporate assets and competitive advantage. Profiling and identifying these skill sets is vital for on-target human capital investing and development. Companies must invest the money where they will make money, and in the era of the knowledge worker, they must strategically strive to outpace (not just keep up with) the competition. This hints at the shift in focus that must take place from just paying people to show up and perform a given function, to investing in people and their development. This strategic shift must go from broad scale spending on training, which may or may not hit the mark and have a bottom-line impact on target, to a *smart bomb* approach. This approach is based on using reconnaissance (i.e., profiling emotional and social skill sets) to tactically select the right targets for maximum effect, minimize off-target collateral damage, and to place no more resources at risk than necessary.

Building high performance teams:

Much of knowledge work will be done in teams and collaborative communities. Who is and what is a *team player* in these new corporate groups? In a recent study conducted by Accountemps of 150 executives from the nation's 1,000 largest companies (*Bottom Line Personal*, September 15, 1997), 37 percent said meeting deadlines was the single most important characteristic of the corporate team player while 20 percent indicated that avoiding office politics is also important, another 20 percent emphasized being pleasant at work, and an additional 17 percent suggested that supporting one's supervisor is a significant attribute as well. In light of these findings, if we were to assemble an automobile like we do today's teams, by merely assembling a collection of roles and functions that the parts represent without considering the fit and desired performance parameters, we would end up with something similar to the Flintstones' automobile. Many teams operate with an emotional and social blind side based on skills skewed towards the analytical and problem-solving mode, but with a personal and interpersonal deficit that leads to the inability to perform the kind of on-the-fly jazz improvisation that will be required of the truly creative high-performance teams. In a sense, the blending, offsetting, and the rounding out of each of the individual players creates a smooth blend of jazz that flows, versus the all-tuba section that blasts away, perhaps making sound, but overpowering the more subtle instruments that need to be heard. By profiling emotional and social skills, a potential team's blind side can be spotted, and team members can be trained in these areas, or other members more skilled in these areas can be added to round out the jazz combo. Besides the obvious performance diagnostic value for teams, composite profiles can be developed from separate team profiles for the organization as a whole, revealing common problems that all may seem to struggle with that can guide organizational intervention. For example, from a large sales and marketing firm profiled by one of the authors, it was learned that the organization as a whole had difficulty with emotional self-awareness, empathy, and interpersonal relationship skills. For an organization in the marketing business, knowing that their weakest attributes are those that should be their strengths had a show-stopping effect on management. Specifically, emotional self-awareness (the ability to be in touch with your own emotions) is critical for empathy (the ability to read others emotions), which impacts your abilities to pick up on social cues and interact with others (interpersonal relationship skills). Needless to say, there were previously no interventions directed at these areas in this organization. However, after receiving this feedback, management quickly began to provide training aimed at improving these skills, which by no accident, had the startling effect (at least to management) of improving organizational performance in their core business competencies.

Guiding organizational restructuring and assessing its impact:

Profiling emotional and social skill sets helps us locate and deploy the right talent where it is needed so that we can stay lean in a downsized environment. The idea, following the business model, is to capitalize and invest in those human capital assets that provide a high rate of return and positive return on investment. Once we have conducted an emotional and social audit, we can start to strategically differentiate those that represent commodity skills, versus true assets. Corporations can then focus their hiring and training strategy to acquire those skill sets in order to amass and concentrate the right talent where it's needed. How much more focused could restructuring be with this type of information versus some of the slash-and-burn tactics we have witnessed in the corporate world. Based on experience received from working with a number of organizations, it frequently comes as a surprise to learn that these skills are truly corporate assets. For example, in a health services organization that one of the authors consulted with, profiling the emotional and social intelligence of the workforce indicated that one of the lowest status groups of employees had the highest interpersonal skills in the whole organization. Interestingly, these employees just so happened to be the ones that interacted the most with the customer; so in a way, they were perhaps the most vital employees to the organization, yet were the least valued within the organization's hierarchy. This illustrates the fallacy of basing restructuring decisions solely on occupational role and position, for it is sometimes those that appear to be the least valuable by this method that are the most valuable when emotional and social skill sets are profiled. Luckily, this specific organization quickly realized the true value of these particular employees and set about a job enrichment initiative to take greater advantage of their "new found" skills worth. Another value of this type of skill set profiling is that it can debunk some traditional myths related to performance. Again, from another study that one of the authors conducted of approximately 1,300 sales and marketing personnel distributed throughout the US, two long-held corporate myths were dismissed. First, it was long held that the geographic region of the country where one was located was the predominant factor associated with high sales performance. Sales quotas and structuring sales territories were at least, in part, based on this long-held maxim. The salespeople thought that it was mostly the luck of the draw with emotional and social skills having very little to do with explaining the differences between high performers and low performers. Based on the results of the emotional and social profiling of this force, it was revealed that the geographic region of the country had no significant statistical connection with high performance. The difference in sales performance was, instead, significantly related to the difference in the emotional and social skills of the performers themselves. Those who scored highest on emotional and social intelligence (EQ) performed the best, regardless of their location. Second, this study refuted yet another performance myth: that the way to increased sales was to put in more hours. The study indicated that those who were the top performers worked the least amount of hours, perhaps due to their more well-developed emotional and social skills that helped them accomplish more in less time. In one sense, this supports the saying, "Work smarter, not harder."

Finally, for those doubters who don't see the value in focusing on the emotional and social profile of their company, the current business literature is replete with stories of how bad-behaving employees hurt the bottom line. One such example is that of the financial havoc wreaked by a manager who threw a tantrum and used some racially disparaging comments resulting in a major lawsuit. Another example is of an employee who was brooding over an imagined slight and withheld vital information causing the loss of a lucrative account. Yet another example is that of an employee who corrupted vital computer files as a means of "getting even" when he was notified of an upcoming rightsizing layoff in his company. These are palpable behaviors. However, imagine the more discreet behaviors, idiosyncrasies, and emotional and social skill deficits of employees who drain their coworkers, subordinates, and bosses of valuable time. We often end up spending 95 percent of our time with those 5 percent of the employees who represent these cases. This is the sort of behavioral, emotional, and social red ink that is ripe for the human capital audit to locate and position its constituents for managing from a true value-added human capital standpoint.

The Importance of Applying Emotional and Social Intelligence in the Workplace

How important is emotional and social intelligence? It is critical to successful functioning in interpersonal relationships at work and elsewhere. This type of intelligence implies the ability to deal with person-to-person relationships and efficient communication. It has real application in the workplace, particularly in customer service, daily coworker relationships, high performance teamwork as well as in leadership and management. Customer service is about person-to-person interaction. Having good emotional and social skills, especially empathy and interpersonal relationship, is requisite for this type of work. This type of intelligence concerns itself with the ability to know not only what you are feeling (emotional self-awareness), but also what others around you are feeling (empathy) and being able to handle both skillfully. But, what has your experience been with most of the customer service representatives that you have come in contact with? The era of the knowledge worker and of human capital is the era of collaborative teams. These teams have to have the ability to be responsive, decisive, flexible, fast-acting, and have a good read on the rapid winds of change, to position their company to act rather than get acted upon. Once again, good emotional and social skills will determine effectiveness in these tasks for many teams. Emotional and social intelligence is also a core competency for any supervisor, manager, or leader. Common sense would tell you that senior managers must possess highly developed interpersonal skills, especially in the intricacies of motivating, understanding, encouraging, coaching, and giving direction, to masterfully get the best out of those who work for them. Once again, what has been your actual experience with people in these positions? Do they possess well-developed emotional and social skills in your opinion?

In conclusion, the message that the reader should take away from all this is that the shift to focus on how best to improve emotional and social intelligence in the workplace, as a way to leverage corporate performance, is not just a passing fad. It is the embodiment of what Doug Englebart envisioned over four decades ago when he spoke about the *co-evolution of human systems with tool systems to enhance the collective IQ* of organizations. Applying emotional and social intelligence in the workplace also appears to exemplify what Peter Drucker may have been referring to when he stressed that *the rise of the knowledge worker will lead to new principles of managing people.* This is also a way for companies to demonstrate a form of management that will allow them to mean it when they say *employees are your most important asset* as Tom Stewart has suggested. With regard to applying emotional and social intelligence in the workplace to improve organizational effectiveness, *learn about it as if the future of your career and your company depends on it.*

INTRODUCTION: Understanding and Improving Emotional and Social Skills at Work

In this chapter, we will define emotional and social intelligence, demonstrate why it is important in the workplace, describe how to evaluate it, and present some basic ideas on how to improve it. The last section of the chapter presents the general outline of this book and how to make the best use of it for improving organizational effectiveness.

Understanding Emotional and Social Intelligence

In order to understand what emotional and social intelligence is, we will first have to define intelligence.

General intelligence is simply *one's overall capacity to think rationally, act purposefully, and to deal effectively with one's environment* (Wechsler, 1958); this includes the ability to adapt to new conditions and to cope with life situations successfully. For the past century, intelligence has been measured with *IQ*, which indicates one's *cognitive* (or mental) capacity and functioning. Cognitive intelligence is basically *the ability to learn new things, recall information, think rationally, apply knowledge, and to solve problems* (Kaplan & Sadock, 1991). General intelligence is composed of two basic parts, or types of intelligence. Cognitive intelligence is an important part of general intelligence but only one part of it; the other part comprises emotional and social knowledge, abilities and skills that are no less important for daily living. The concept of emotional and social intelligence (or noncognitive intelligence to be exact) brings new depth to understanding what *is* intelligent behavior and increases our ability to evaluate and improve general intelligence. Like cognitive intelligence, noncognitive intelligence is not easy to define; most of the definitions are either too narrow and specific or too general and vague.

Noncognitive (emotional and social) intelligence is defined here as *an array of emotional, personal, and social abilities and skills that influence one's overall ability to succeed in coping with environmental demands and pressures.* As such, this represents an important factor in determining one's ability to succeed in life and directly influences one's general emotional health. This is called the "Bar-On model" and is considered to be the most comprehensive and operational model of emotional and social intelligence that exists today (Bar-On, 1998). The factorial components, or building blocks, of this model that are measured by the EQ-i (Bar-On, 1996a) are listed below:

Intrapersonal Components	Interpersonal Components	Stress Mgt. Components
Self-Regard	Empathy	Stress Tolerance
Emotional Self-Awareness	Social Responsibility	Impulse Control
Assertiveness	Interpersonal Relationship	Independence
Self-Actualization		

Adaptability Components	General Mood Components
Reality Testing	Optimism
Flexibility	Happiness
Problem Solving	

The Bar-On Model focuses on the key emotional and social abilities and skills upon which the potential for performance is based. It is process-oriented and designed to predict one's ability to effectively and successfully deal with daily demands. These fifteen abilities and skills will be defined and described in detail in the next five chapters.

Some Hard Core Reasons Why EQ is a Powerful Predictor of Effective and Successful Performance

There is a wealth of research findings (Bar-On, 1997a) that demonstrate that EQ is a powerful predictor of effective and successful performance in the workplace and in other areas of life. Presented below are some of the results related to successful performance based on our research.

Based on a recent article in the *American Psychologist* (Wagner, 1997), years of accumulated data on the ability of IQ to predict job performance suggest that cognitive intelligence accounts for only 6 percent of one's ability to succeed in the workplace. This means that IQ is a rather poor predictor of occupational success. In contrast to these findings, EQ has shown to account for approximately 27 percent of job performance based on research conducted in this area (Bar-On, 1998). These results clearly indicate that EQ is a better predictor of occupational and professional performance than IQ.

In a research project conducted by Multi-Health Systems in Toronto, approximately 8,140 people were administered the EQ-i in North America and then asked how successful they felt they were at work. They were divided into those who felt that their performance was successful and those who thought that they were not successful. Those who were considered to be more successful demonstrated significantly higher EQ scores than those who felt that they were less successful in their work. The more successful people were significantly higher in *self-actualization, optimism, self-regard, happiness, stress tolerance*, and *problem solving*.

In the first study of its kind comparing a group of people's IQ and EQ scores with a measure of job performance, a graduate psychology student

(Hee-Woo, 1998), has demonstrated that emotional and social intelligence is significantly and highly correlated (.52) with job performance while cognitive intelligence has shown a very low and insignificant correlation (.07) with performance in the workplace. While the importance of noncognitive intelligence in job performance has been the subject of speculation over the past few years, this is the first scientific study that has proven that EQ is more important than IQ. This shows that the truly intelligent human being is one who is not only *cogtelligent* (cognitively intelligent) but *emtelligent* (emotionally and socially intelligent) as well.

In another study (Handley, 1997), carried out in the US Armed Forces, the relationship was examined between EQ scores and the ability of Air Force recruiters to fill their recruitment quotas (which equates to job performance). EQ accounted for 45 percent of success in this study that included 1,171 recruiters worldwide. Specific areas were identified as key factors in successful recruiting, which parallel other studies carried out on salespeople requiring similar skills. In addition to a significantly higher overall EQ score, the best performing recruiters scored high on *assertiveness*, *flexibility*, *problem solving*, *stress tolerance*, and *optimism*. Based on these results, the Air Force altered their recruitment procedures for selecting recruiters and, thus, increased the accuracy of their ability to successfully select the right people with the right stuff by almost three times.

In a third study, which was recently conducted by Multi-Health Systems in Toronto, a group of engineers were also tested with the Bar-On EQ-i and independently evaluated regarding their job performance. Based on the results, EQ was able to significantly predict *star performers*. This study also suggests that EQ can play a significant role in helping to select high performers. General adaptability was the best predictor of these high-performing engineers, accounting for 25 percent of job performance. The specific abilities and skills that significantly distinguish between the average and high performers are efficient *reality testing*, *flexibility*, *stress tolerance*, *impulse control*, and *optimism*.

In another interesting study conducted by Multi-Health Systems (Bar-On, 1997a), the Sense of Competence Questionnaire was administered along with the EQ-i to a sample of 324 individuals in the United States and Canada. The sample included university students and individuals from various professions on the staff of two large general hospitals. The total

SCQ score, which gives a good estimate of a self-perceived sense of job competence, highly correlated (.56) with the total EQ score accounting for 31 percent of job performance. Those factors that significantly differentiated high performers from low performers were *self-regard, emotional self-awareness, independence, self-actualization, reality testing, problem solving, stress tolerance, impulse control*, and *happiness*.

In a study designed to examine the role played by emotional and social intelligence in coping with occupational stress (Bar-On, 1997a), 862 adults were asked to complete both the EQ-i and the Coping Inventory for Stressful Situations. It was clearly shown that a task-oriented coping style is positively linked with adaptive and healthy behavior. This demonstrated the positive relationship between emotional and social intelligence and effective coping. The most important emotional and social skills involved in successfully coping with occupational stress are positive and effective *self-regard, assertiveness, self-actualization, problem solving, stress tolerance,* and *optimism*.

Not only was it scientifically demonstrated that EQ is significantly related to job performance, but a number of findings have shown that job satisfaction is also related to emotional and social intelligence. In one such study (Bar-On, 1997a), the EQ-i and a job satisfaction questionnaire was administered to a North American sample of 314 participants in order to assess the degree of association between EQ variables and one's ability to be satisfied with one's work. The participants tested came from a variety of occupations and professions including salespersons, teachers, college students, nurses, and so forth. The Work Satisfaction Questionnaire (constructed specifically for this study) provides a total work satisfaction score that can be divided into the ability to derive satisfaction from work and physical aspects of the work (like working conditions, working hours, job security, salary, and so forth). Fairly good relationships were found between the EQ-i scales and work satisfaction. Specifically, the following EQ factors appear to be the most important in predicting job satisfaction: *emotional self-awareness, self-regard, self-actualization, social responsibility, reality testing,* and *optimism*. These factors contribute to approximately 20 percent of our ability to predict how satisfied one will be their work.

Not only is EQ an important factor in job performance and satisfaction, but additional research findings suggest that emotional and social intelligence is important in predicting academic performance. A study conducted in South Africa (Swart, 1996) supports this assumption. The EQ scores of 448 first-year university students were compared with the grades they received at the end of their first year. It was found that those students who received higher grades were those who were assessed as being more emotionally and socially intelligent. In addition to a significantly higher total EQ score, the following emotional and social factors were able to clearly differentiate the more successful students from the less successful: *self-actualization*, *reality testing*, *problem solving*, *stress tolerance*, and *optimism*. Overall the high academic performers were more adaptable and coped better with stress than the rest. All in all, this study demonstrates that people who are more successful academically have significantly higher EQ. The results suggest that an important factor in predicting academic success is emotional and social intelligence.

Another study that examined the connection between EQ and academic performance was conducted on 1,000 first-year students in a North American military academy (Bar-On, 1997a). They were given the EQ-i and asked to rate how successful they felt they were in their studies. For the most part, the results suggest that people who perceive themselves as being more successful have significantly higher emotional and social intelligence than people who feel less successful. These results suggest that emotional and social intelligence is significantly related to self-perceived success. In addition to a significantly higher total EQ score, the following factors are the most relevant: *self-regard*, *self-actualization*, *stress tolerance*, and *optimism*.

Not only is emotional and social intelligence associated with job performance and the ability of to derive satisfaction from work, but it is also related to satisfaction from one's marital life. In one study (Handley, 1997), 1,119 people were asked how satisfied they were with their marriage. In addition to having a significantly higher overall EQ score, those who indicated that they were more satisfied with their marriage revealed significantly higher scores on *happiness*, *self-regard*, *emotional self-awareness*, *self-actualization*, *reality testing*, *interpersonal relationship*, *social responsibility*, and *optimism*.

One of the interesting things about emotional and social intelligence is its ability to predict efficient and successful performance in many different aspects of life like school, work, and family life. However, this is not surprising in that the Bar-On model of noncognitive intelligence was developed to describe the key emotional, personal, and social abilities that determine one's ability to efficiently cope with various types of *environmental demands*. For example, EQ was found to significantly correlate with acculturation when the EQ-i was administered to a group of new immigrants in the United States (Garrido, 1996). Acculturation is essentially adjustment to the different cultural traits and social patterns of another human environment, which often places a very stressful environmental demand on people. The results revealed that EQ was able to significantly differentiate between immigrants who were more successful from immigrants who were less successful at acculturating. These results represent an additional indication that the Bar-On model is capable of tapping one's ability to cope with environmental demands and pressures (i.e., emotional and social intelligence).

Another example of emotional and social intelligence being able to predict efficient and successful functioning is related to health issues. Multi-Health Systems in Toronto asked 3,829 individuals in the US and Canada how well they generally cope with serious health problems. Once again, it was found that those people with higher EQ cope significantly better than those with lower emotional and social intelligence. The key factors related to one's ability to cope with health problems are *stress tolerance, optimism, flexibility, self-regard, reality testing*, and *assertiveness*.

In another interesting study comparing one's emotional and social intelligence with the ability to deal with serious health problems, a graduate student administered the EQ-i to fifty-eight people in South Africa within ten days of suffering a myocardial infarct (Dunkley, 1996). Suffering a heart attack was considered to be a very difficult and stressful experience that one would have to cope with. The results indicated that the cardiac patients have significantly lower EQ scores than the normal population. However, it is difficult to say whether this is due to the fact that *potential* cardiac patients prior to suffering a heart attack possess lower emotional and social intelligence than the normal population or that the differences occur because of the individuals' reaction to this serious medical condition. This clinical sample was then divided into two groups. One group participated in a brief stress management program, and the other did not. The program included simple instructions on how to better identify stressful situations resulting in anxiety and ways to better cope with this condition. The EQ-i was administered to both groups within ten days after suffering the heart attack, as was previously stated, and once again after the one group completed the stress management program. Those patients who participated in the program received significantly higher EQ scores than those who did not. In addition to the overall EQ score, the greatest difference was revealed on the following factors: *self-regard, assertiveness, reality testing, flexibility, problem solving, stress tolerance,* and *happiness.*

In another study conducted in South Africa, a graduate student in psychology administered the EQ-i to sixty-seven people at the onset of treatment in a substance abuse center for alcoholics (Flett, 1996). At the end of an intensive rehabilitation program, the EQ-i was re-administered to the same group of people. Those who responded better to the program were those who received higher EQ scores. The key factors that differentiated the two groups were *self-regard, social responsibility, interpersonal relationship, reality testing, flexibility, problem solving, stress tolerance,* and *impulse control.* These results suggest that EQ can predict one's ability to benefit from rehabilitation programs designed to treat substance abuse patients.

An additional approach to examining the relationship between emotional and social intelligence and the ability to cope with environmental demands and pressures was carried out on psychiatric patients. The differences on EQ scores between four different clinical samples in four countries and matched normative samples in those countries were studied. These subjects included outpatients in South Africa (Bar-On, 1988) and the US (Pallazza & Bar-On, 1995), inpatients in Israel (Shevetz, Stir, & Bar-On, 1996), and a mixture of outpatients and inpatients in Argentina (Dupertuis, 1996). The results revealed significant differences in EQ between the clinical and matched samples in the four countries. This, once again, demonstrates the ability of EQ to differentiate among individuals who are more successful and less successful in coping with environmental demands and pressures. It appears that people who succeed in maintaining emotional health are primarily those who possess higher emotional and social intelligence. Those emotional and social factors that cross-culturally surface as the most powerful determinants of emotional health are *self-regard*, *reality testing*, *stress tolerance*, and *happiness*.

One of the authors and Multi-Health Systems in Toronto are presently engaged in an effort to develop a comprehensive list of EQ profiles for various occupational and professional groups. Eventually, this effort will lead to the publication of a handbook that will allow users to quickly locate, for example, the EQ profile for successful insurance salespeople, firefighters, and senior managers. Such profiles can be created for not only various occupational groups in general but for those specific occupations in a particular organization. This type of material will provide valuable information for recruiting and selecting *the right people with the right stuff* and then continuing their in-house training.

Below is a brief sample of the EQ profiles for successful individuals in eight corporate occupations and professions. It is important to stress that these profiles were scientifically developed based on research findings from a number of studies conducted on thousands of people.

Salespeople: The more successful members of this group have significantly well-developed interpersonal skills. More specifically, they exhibit more empathy and are more successful in relating with people than others. Moreover, the more successful in this occupation have a stronger sense of self and are more able to assert their feelings and ideas than others.

Insurance Agents: The more successful members of this group have significantly well-developed interpersonal skills and intrapersonal capacity. In addition to demonstrating greater empathy and ability to relate well with others, as well as possessing a stronger sense of self and being able to assert themselves better than others, the more successful in this group are more optimistic and better able to tolerate stress than others.

Customer Service Reps: The more successful members of this group show more empathy and concern for others, relate better with people, can withstand stress better, and are more able to adjust to different situations and solve problems better than other individuals.

Marketing Professionals: In general, the more successful members of this group are stronger intrapersonally, more adaptable, and more highly motivated than others. More specifically, they have a stronger sense of self, can express their feelings and ideas better, are more independent, and have a greater ability to actualize their potential and accomplish what they want to accomplish more than others. Additionally, they are better at flexibly sizing up the immediate situation and more optimistic about doing what they do than other individuals are.

Public Relations Consultants: The successful members of this group possess significantly greater interpersonal skills and are more motivated in general than others. The more successful members of this group demonstrate greater empathy and concern for others and are better in establishing and maintaining contact with people than others. Moreover, they are more optimistic and better at sizing up the immediate situation than other people.

Human Resources Consultants: The successful members of this group have significantly more well-developed intrapersonal capacity and are more motivated than others. More specifically, they are more aware of themselves, have a stronger sense of self, are more able to assert their feelings and ideas, and are more satisfied with their ability to accomplish what they attempt to accomplish. Moreover, the more successful in this occupation are more optimistic in general and optimistic in their ability to withstand stress than others.

Employment Counselors: The interpersonal skills of the more successful members of this group are more significantly well developed than others. More specifically, they reveal a significantly higher ability to understand their own feelings and those of others and are able to relate better with people than others. Additionally they stand out as being optimistic in general and more able to accurately and efficiently size up the immediate situation.

Senior Managers: The more successful senior managers have a significantly higher intrapersonal capacity, are more adaptable, and are better at managing stress than others. More specifically, they have an exceptionally strong sense of self, are independent, and are able to assert their feelings and ideas much better and quicker than many other people. Moreover, they are significantly more flexible and more able to confidently and optimistically handle stress than other people.

At the other extreme, EQ-i data were collected from a sample of 250 chronically unemployed individuals representing a group that is at the opposite end of the continuum of occupational success. When compared with an employed population sample of close to 10,000 individuals, they exhibited significantly lower EQ scores. The chronically unemployed sample was especially weak in inner strength and adaptability. The lowest scores for this sample appeared in *assertiveness*, *reality testing*, and *happiness*. Scores were also below average in *self-regard* and *independence*. These results may very well explain their lack of success in finding and maintaining a job. A continued lack of success in this area may reinforce and help to maintain these under-developed emotional and social skills, thereby creating a chronic situation. Once again, these results clearly demonstrate the ability of emotional and social intelligence to differentiate people who are successful from those who are unsuccessful in coping with environmental demands and pressure.

Other research results that are important to note are those related to gender and age differences.

There are no differences between males and females regarding overall EQ. However, significant gender differences do exist for a few factorial components of emotional and social intelligence. Based on a North American study (Bar-On, 1997a) of close to 2,000 males and approximate-ly 2,000 females from late adolescence to late adulthood, females seem to have stronger interpersonal skills than males, but the latter have a higher intrapersonal capacity, are more adaptable, and are better at stress management. More specifically, women are more aware of their emotions, show more empathy, relate better interpersonally, and act more socially responsible than men; men appear to have better self-regard, are more independent, solve problems better, are more flexible, and cope better with stress than women. Similar significant differences related to interpersonal relationship, social responsibility, and stress tolerance between males and females have been observed in almost every other population sample that has been examined around the world to date.

Based on the above-mentioned North American population sample, the age effects show numerous significant differences between younger and older individuals although these differences are small. Older people scored signifi-cantly higher in EQ than the younger people, and the 40- to 49-year-old age group demonstrated the highest scores. These results suggest that emotional and intelligence increases with age and, thus, changes throughout life. This finding is very interesting when one takes into account that cognitive intelli-gence remains relatively stable from about seventeen years of age and onward.

How to Evaluate EQ

We will be referring to two methods of evaluating EQ in the workplace. The first method of evaluating emotional and social intelligence that is discussed is the Bar-On Emotional Quotient Inventory or simply the EQ-i (Bar-On, 1996a); this is the most accurate and scientific way of assessing the EQ of individuals and organizations. Secondly, the SWOT analysis is employed throughout this book as a basis to understanding and improving EQ in the workplace. Both methods of evaluating and understanding EQ are combined to form a basis for improving emotional and social intelligence to improve organizational effectiveness.

The EQ-i Assessment Method:

The EQ-i is based on the Bar-On conceptual model of emotional and social intelligence and was specifically constructed to measure this concept. It is the first and most comprehensive test of emotional, personal, and social intelligence to be published; it is published by Multi-Health Systems in Toronto. The published version of the Bar-On EQ-i is composed of 133 brief items and employs a five-point response format ranging from "very seldom or not true of me" to "very often true of me or true of me." It takes an average of forty minutes to complete this inventory. The reading level in English has been assessed at the North American sixth grade level. The EQ-i is suitable for individuals 17 years of age and older; two additional versions of the inventory are presently being developed for children from 6 to 12 and for adolescents from 13 to 17 years of age. The EQ-i t renders a *Total EQ* score and the following five EQ composite scale scores based on fifteen subscale scores:

1. Intrapersonal EQ (based on Self-Regard, Emotional Self-Awareness, Assertiveness, Independence, and Self-Actualization),
2. Interpersonal EQ (based on Empathy, Social Responsibility, and Interpersonal Relationship),
3. Adaptability EQ (based on Reality Testing, Flexibility, and Problem Solving),
4. Stress Management EQ (based on Stress Tolerance and Impulse Control), and

5. General Mood EQ (based on Optimism and Happiness).

The scores are computer-generated, and the results are displayed in numeric, verbal, and graphic fashion followed by a textural report. Average to above average scores on the EQ-i indicate an emotionally and socially healthy, well-functioning, and efficient individual (i.e., one who is emotionally and socially intelligent). The higher the scores, the more positive the prediction for effective functioning in meeting environmental demands and pressures. On the other hand, an inability to succeed in life and the possible existence of emotional problems are suggested by low scale scores on this inventory. Moreover, low scores on the following scales should be considered more problematic for coping with one's environment: *Reality Testing, Problem Solving, Stress Tolerance,* and *Impulse Control.*

Interpretive Guidelines for Bar-On EQ-i Scale Scores

Standard Score	Interpretive Guideline
130+	*Markedly High*—atypically well-developed emotional and social capacity ("Strengths")
120–129	*Very High*—extremely well-developed emotional and social capacity ("Strengths")
110–119	*High*—well-developed emotional and social capacity ("Strengths")
90–109	*Average*—effective emotional and social capacity ("Opportunities")

Standard Score	Interpretive Guideline
80–89	*Low*—underdeveloped emotional and social capacity ("Weaknesses")
70–79	*Very Low*—extremely underdeveloped emotional and social capacity ("Threats")
Under 70	*Markedly Low* — atypically underdeveloped emotional and social capacity

The SWOT Approach in Understanding and Improving EQ in the Workplace:

The following five sections of this book employ the SWOT format when discussing how to best understand and improve the fifteen factorial components of emotional and social intelligence in the workplace. The SWOT analysis is an analytical tool frequently used by strategic planners in the business world. SWOT stands for *Strengths, Weaknesses, Opportunities*, and *Threats*. The analysis of strengths and weaknesses is typically used by companies aimed at examining the organization's strong and weak points and their impact on being able to compete effectively. Strengths are the positive aspects internal to the organization, and weaknesses are the negative aspects internal to the organization. In applying the SWOT analysis to understanding and improving EQ in the workplace, we begin by first examining the *internal* aspects of the organization (its strengths and weaknesses). When we examine the *strengths* of the organization, we are asking: What are the existing emotional and social skills that are well-developed and well-functioning? Strengths are revealed by scores that are equal to or greater than 110 on the EQ-i, indicating well-developed emotional and social capacity and functioning. The SWOT approach to understanding your strengths can simply be done by examining each of the fifteen areas and their definitions and thought-fully noting your strong points in a realistic manner from your point of view (internal), and then shifting to the point of view of others (external). Are there things you are confident with that others don't see, and conversely, are there things that others see about you that you don't? Obviously, if you or your organization has taken the EQ-i, you will already know which areas you are strong or weak in. The second aspect of orga-nizational assessment focuses on examining potential *weaknesses*. What are the areas that you should improve? Once again, it is recommended to use an internal-external perspective when you examine your organiza-tion's potential weaknesses. First, ask what areas are you aware of and then shift to asking what are the areas that you feel your close acquain-tances will most likely say that you are weak in. The idea here is that we frequently see our strengths but don't always see weaknesses that others may more easily pick up. Realistically facing an unpleasant truth now is far better than having it haunt us at a later more critical juncture. Weaknesses are revealed by scores that range from 80 to 89 on the EQ-i, indicating underdeveloped emotional and social capacity and functioning. *Opportunities* are frequently thought of as positive aspects that exist *external* to the organization. Analyzing opportunity is typically focused on the organization's external competitive environment and the opportunities presented by the marketplace. Within the EQ framework, these represent the opportunities for improving those skills that we are weak in and suggestions as to how you might begin this process. Opportunities are revealed by scores that range from 90 to 109 on the EQ-i, indicating effective emotional and social capacity and functioning. *Threats* are typically thought of as the negative aspects external to the organization. These again are typically thought of in terms of the competitive environment and the threats an organization might face in the marketplace. Threats are revealed by scores that are equal to or less than 80 on the EQ-i, indicating extremely underdeveloped capacity and functioning. Within the framework of the Bar-On model, threats are associated with significant weaknesses in one of the areas of emotional and social intelligence or associated with weaknesses in several combined areas. For example, a weakness in reality testing is one thing, but when it is combined with weaknesses in problem solving and impulse control, the threat to the individual and the organization is greater and more severe. This troublesome combination could create serious problems in accurately assessing situations, avoiding impulsive moves, and in generating multiple solutions to solving problems. Finally, the SWOT format is laid out from an individual and organizational perspective: what it means from an individual view in terms of strengths, weaknesses, opportunities, and threats with regard to EQ, and what it means for an organization as a whole.

Some Basic Ideas on How to Give Effective Feedback Designed to Improve Corporate EQ

Giving feedback related to emotional and social intelligence is very important for individuals and organizations alike. As was previously stated, this provides the basis for the emotional audit that can be used to improve organizational effectiveness. However, merely providing this feedback is not enough, nor is it enough to just provide the "what to do" without the skills and authority to do it. In a recent survey cited in the *Wall Street Journal* (August 1997) of 9,144 workers conducted by Watson Wyatt Worldwide in Bethesda Maryland, over 80 percent of the respondents said they know their employer's goals. However, only 38 percent of these respondents felt they receive performance *feedback* on a regular basis, and only 55 percent noted they had the power to make the necessary decisions to perform their tasks at work. Though giving feedback to employees is an essential part of management, when it is poorly done it usually has a destructive effect. Employees become de-motivated and their performance actually drops when criticism is inconsiderate and general (e.g., "You don't do anything right!"). Emotionally and socially intelligent managers are sufficiently empathetic to phrase and direct their criticism in such a way as to get the desired results (e.g., "You're really good at drafting sales proposals, but I would like to work with you more on your presentation skills"). The general approach in giving feedback should be informative, to the point, positive, constructive, and encouraging. The person receiving feedback should be convinced that this is an important and valuable opportunity to learn about themselves and improve themselves. The way that managers treat subordinates has a powerful influence on their behavior. J. Sterling Livingston's discussion of the influence of self-fulfilling prophecies and the "Pygmalion effect" (*Harvard Business Review*, 1988) exemplifies this point quite clearly. Pygmalion was a sculptor in Greek mythology who carved a statue of a beautiful woman. He literally worshipped the statue and wished it would come to life. The legend has it that the goddess Venus took pity on Pygmalion and brought the statue Galitea to life. The notion that one person can transform another was the basis for Livingston's article. He documents a well-illustrated example of the impact of managerial expectations on performance by citing Alfred Oberlander's 1961 study. Oberlander, who was the manager of the Rockaway district office of the Metropolitan Life Insurance Company, noticed that new agents performed better when placed in high-producing agencies than in average or poor agencies. He grouped the superior agents and trained new agents in this environment. The results were higher performance by the superior group, but performance decline in the poor-performing group. He concluded that the performance of the high-potential agents increased due to the expectations of the managers, just as the low performers performed to manager expectations. Interestingly, the middle group of managers performed at a higher level than expected. This was primarily due to the fact that the manager of this group refused to believe that she was only an average manager and, hence, motivated her people to believe they had high potential. Her treatment and expectations (Pygmalion effect) resulted in their performing at a higher level than what was expected by the district management. This group displayed confidence in its own abilities, the so-called "Galitea effect," and the performance boost was partially due to the rise in the worker's own self-expectations.

The influence of managers' expectations on their subordinates' behavior and performance does have limits. There must be a balance between challenging and attainable expectations. Berlew and Hall noted that placing expectations that are seen as virtually certain or as impossible to attain yield limited motivation to achieve (Berlew & Hall, 1966). Second, if personnel fail to meet expectations that are close to their own expectations, they will lower their performance standards and develop negative attitudes toward the task or job.

While some managers are able to produce high levels of performance by combining attainable expectations with effective feedback and skillful coaching, others seem unable to motivate their subordinates. It has been found that superior managers tend to have greater confidence in their own ability to develop the talent of their subordinates, which is often based on what the managers think of themselves and expect of themselves. They strongly believe in their ability to select, train, and motivate their subordinates. These beliefs seem to subtly influence their subordinates' behavior and to lend credibility to their high expectations of them, which are viewed as realistic and attainable.

Rosenthal and Jacobsen (1968) identified four management-related factors that positively influence the performance of subordinates. First, successful managers are able to promote the development of a warm, supportive, and accepting climate. Second, they can stimulate high performance by providing frequent and specific feedback that focuses on what the subordinate is doing right. The goal is to assist the subordinate in developing more competence and self-confidence. Third, successful managers should provide all the necessary resources to enhance the skills of subordinates and allow them to effectively complete tasks. Finally, managers should support the attempts of subordinates by promoting innovative and creative approaches, accepting mistakes during experimentation, and providing assistance in problem solving.

The ideas presented above point to the need for organizations to rethink the influence of expectations on performance. This permeates the entire organizational and employment life cycle from recruitment to retirement. The most important part of the employment life cycle is the first few months that employees spend with an organization. The first manager is usually the most influential in their career. These managers must be willing to meet all four of the aforementioned conditions and play a powerful part in mentoring and developing the greatest potential weapon the organization has in the era of intellectual capital: its own talent pool. As Eliza Doolittle, in George Bernard Shaw's *Pygmalion*, explains: "The difference between a lady and a flower girl is not in how she behaves, but in how she's treated."

Finally, consistent and effective feedback from top management on down goes a long way in helping create a sense of strategic shared vision, dispelling rumors, and giving people the big picture outlook. A recent study cited in *Management Review* by Quinn Spitzer, CEO, Kepner-Tregoe Management Consultants indicated that 57 percent of line employees and 49 percent of middle managers don't understand the decisions made by top management. Further, 39 percent of line employees and 29 percent of middle managers aren't clear about their responsibilities in solving problems and making decisions, and 40 percent of managers say their companies don't provide adequate training to develop the skills that employees need to succeed on the job.

Frederick Herzberg (1968) indicated that the growth or *motivator* factors that motivate employees intrinsic to the job are achievement, recognition for this achievement, the work itself (meaningful work), responsibility, and the opportunity for growth and advancement. He noted that the dissatisfaction or *hygiene* factors extrinsic to the job included company policy and administration, supervision, interpersonal relationships, working conditions, salary, status, and security. Basically, Herzberg pointed to the fact that the *motivators* were the primary cause for job satisfaction, and the *hygiene* factors were the major cause of unhappiness on the job. It is noteworthy that Herzberg differentiates between *movement* and *motivation*. *Movement* is seen more as a function of fear of punishment or failure to get extrinsic rewards. The down side of movement is that, in the long term, it requires constant reinforcement and stresses short-term results. *Motivation*, on the other hand, is a function of growth from getting intrinsic rewards from work that is viewed as interesting and challenging. Motivation is based more on growth needs, which is an *internal engine* of sorts producing its benefits over a long period of time, obviously because of the ultimate reward, which is personal growth. People don't have to be rewarded incrementally. The key of Herzberg's *Motivation-Hygiene Theory* is job enrichment, which is designing work that motivates employees. Movement, compared to what will be required to compete in the global era of knowledge-based work, is *sterile*. In contrast, *motivation* encompasses *passion*. The challenge, to piggyback on Warren Bennis's book title *Organizing Genius — The Secrets of Creative Collaboration*, is to get the best from your people, creating truly *great groups*, implanting them with infectious optimism and the belief that they can do anything.

Jim Miller (1996) offers some solid insights for coaching in the workplace that are consistent with Livingston's *Pygmalion* and Herzberg's *Motivation Hygiene Theory* aimed at helping employees grow, develop positive self-regard, and feel good about themselves. Ultimately this contributes to a work environment where employee self-esteem is high.

Great coaches must:

- Learn to admit "I made a mistake."
- Learn to say "You did a good job."
- Learn to ask "If you please."
- Learn to express "Thank you."
- Learn that the most important word is "we" and that the least important word is "I."

Some other basic insights offered by Miller are the following:

- Hire people as smart or smarter than you are (which follows the analogy of great sports teams: you can't win if you don't have the right players).
- Coaches must be clear about the organizational and team goals: clarity about what each team member's contribution is expected to be, and what standards will be used to measure their performance.

- Listen and be flexible and responsive to your people — listening connotes a sense of validation to the insights of each person. If we are not able to make changes, we owe it to them to explain "why."
- Trust and empower your people — trust is fundamental to high performance and includes giving people the power to make decisions in their domain and backs them up.
- Recognize employees for their performance, learn to say "thank you" and be honest with them — it is said that the majority of communication is "validate me" messages and that most behavior is "goal-directed behavior" with the frequent goal being to seek attention and approval from significant others.

From behavioral science, we learn that behavior that is reinforced is likely to be repeated. The old saying about parenting your child applies here: "catch them being good." Secondly, be honest and behave with integrity. When we learn to tell the truth, we don't have to remember what we said. The point to be made here is that we indeed weave a *tangled web* when we practice to deceive. We lose credibility when we do this and have a hard time asking our subordinates to "don't do as I do, do as I say do." In this regard, one of the most powerful things we can do is to honestly admit when we have made a mistake, especially when it is the basis for behavior expected of a subordinate. One of the co-authors was involved in facilitating a session between a number of angry subordinates and their boss. The gist of their anger was not knowing why the boss had changed a rule that previously was "okay" for them to do. When the boss was asked point blank, his words instantly defused their anger and rendered them speechless, because he had done the unexpected. He simply said that the reason that he changed the rule was "because I did not want you to do what I had been doing which was wrong." He went on to note how it had led to a struggle and public failure on his part and that he didn't want them to possibly struggle with the same. These words were so powerful and unexpected that the room became dead silent, and their anger turned into renewed respect for the credibility of the "boss."

Bottom Line Recommendations:

- Nothing succeeds like success. New personnel must get a taste very early of what success feels, smells, and tastes like primarily through being a part of a successful team. There is no replacement — set them up for success.

- Managers must walk the walk and talk the talk. Management by personal example is powerful. If the leader has a self-fulfilling prophecy of doom and gloom, why should the subordinates be any different. Additionally, remember that when you point one finger, there are three pointing back at you. Avoid the hypocrisy of holding others to a standard that you don't even meet yourself.

- Great leaders refuse to accept the conventional judgments about what they can't achieve, they just make it happen. It is said that scientists have studied the bumblebee, and theoretically it shouldn't be able to fly. The problem is that no one told the bumblebee this.

- Leadership is about relationship. Great coaches know their charges to the intimate degree. They to know when to push to get more out of their charges, and when to throttle them back.

- Every leader in the organization, from the CEO on down, should be involved in mentoring the talent pool of their organization, especially new personnel. This is the discipling that has to take place to develop the kind of talent that will turn the world upside down. So, be careful as to the model of who you expose your people to.

- Senior management on down must provide consistent, effective communication aimed at encouraging a sense of shared strategic vision and developing a big picture outlook. In this regard, morale, esprit de corps, and group cohesiveness tend to increase in relationship to the degree that leaders are visible in the individual work areas and provide their people access to them. Before making strategic personnel restructuring decisions, especially those involving potential adverse actions, spend some time in immersion. Immerse yourself in their world, even if only for a few hours. Putting yourself in their shoes gives you the minimum requisite insight to make these decisions, especially when the destinies of others are in your hands. It also helps when leaders have to make decisions with regard to work quality-of-life issues. It goes a long way for employees to know that the boss knows how hot it is in the warehouse and what we put up with because he or she has been here, worked a few hours with us, and knows our plight.

A suggested model for giving feedback:

- First, describe the event you are concerned about in behavioral, inquisitive terms: "I was wondering if you could help me understand the episode I witnessed today between Bob and yourself?"
- Second, relate your interpretation of this behavior in a nonthreatening, inquisitive manner: "It seemed to me that you were very angry and raised your voice when dealing with him?"
- Third, allow for feedback since you obviously are not a mind reader, might not have all the facts, and may want to clarify your perception before you arrive at a belief about the situation: "You are right, I did get angry and raise my voice, but what you didn't see was that Bob had just previously inappropriately touched me!"
- Fourth, empathetically reflect meaning with this adjusted insight: "I'm sorry I was unaware of that. I understand now that your behavior meant that you felt threatened or humiliated and treated inappropriately."

By focusing on the Event-Interpretation-Feedback-Meaning model when giving feedback, we focus on the behavior and avoid attacking the person. Finally, the purpose of feedback is to shape the behavior, not break the spirit.

Greater Tolerance:

Today's work environment is becoming increasingly diverse and this trend is expected to continue. Though diversity can bring new opportunities, people's stereotypes and prejudices can cause severe problems. For example, capable, high-performing individuals may be passed over for promotion merely because of prejudice. Emotionally and socially intelligent people are able to recognize their stereotypes and eradicate them or minimize their impact. Peter Drucker, perhaps the most perceptive observer of leadership of our time, defines "intellectual integrity" as *the ability to see the world as it is, not as you want it to be* (*Forbes*, March 10, 1997). There Drucker's own description of himself as a "social ecologist" who was "born to see and meant to look" calls for the need to see beyond the external outward appearance and into the very heart of every matter, issue, and person. In a sense, seeing past the prejudices, judgments, and supposed capabilities of persons to what they have the capability to be, and making that happen. A great story to illustrate this was featured in *Look Magazine* in the 1960s entitled "Sweeney's Miracle." It detailed the story of Professor James Sweeney, who taught industrial management and psychiatry at Tulane University and was also in charge of the Biomedical Computer Center. He believed it was possible to teach an uneducated person, by the name of George Johnson, to operate the computer and, hence, invested himself in teaching a poorly educated janitor to be a computer operator. Others were quick to pass judgment on this person as not having the minimum IQ to operate the computer, and the stereotype that he was a member of a minority group and just a lowly janitor had to play into this case. Sweeney threatened to resign unless Johnson was given the chance. Not only did he learn the computer, he learned it so well that he was eventually put in charge of the main computer room. Sweeney's expectations and confidence in his own ability to teach and George's true ability to learn to be a computer operator led to this fulfillment of his beliefs and "Sweeney's Miracle."

Some More Bottom Line Recommendations:

- Have the intellectual integrity to see things, situations, and people for what they really are, not through imposing your own personal beliefs upon them.
- It's far easier to tear a house down than to build it up. It takes greater skill as a manager and business leader to be a Professor Sweeney who defied conventional wisdom to empower an individual to live at a level commensurate with his true capability.
- Leaders owe it to themselves and their subordinates to "ask not what they can do for you, but for what you can do for them."
- Success always comes on the backs of other people. Will Rogers indicated that you have to "dance with the one that brung ya." Never underestimate who really brung ya. Even those personnel occupying positions that traditional stereotypes place little value upon are of

importance to the organization.

- Seriously consider Peter Drucker's description of himself as a social ecologist who looks out the window to see what's visible but not yet seen. Every situation and person is a window to what is visible through our own preset assumptions and personal beliefs, or a window to the visible but not yet seen.

Team Skills:

The diversified nature of work often means that no one person can complete a job alone. People must work with other people to get the job done, through formal and informal teams. Bell Labs studied what makes certain people *stars* at getting their work done faster and better than their colleagues. Neither (cognitive) intelligence nor personality differentiated the average performer from the high performer. It was the high performer's ability to use informal networks and contacts that let them achieve spectacularly. People with low EQ, especially regarding interpersonal skills, just can't compete with a person who has a large network of friends, colleagues, and experts backing him or her up. This skill is essential for knowledge work, as much of it takes place in teams and collaborative communities of practice. The analogy that two heads are better than one stumbles a bit when we seek to apply it *carte blanche* to team performance. Sometimes, people who are individually smart arrive at fabulously dumb decisions when put into groups. Spitzer and Evans (1997) raise an arresting question: How did the past greats of American business, often without degrees, without the benefit of the latest management fad of our time, manage to stay in business? The bottom line is that they were great at a basic skill called problem solving. Second, Bennis and Biederman (1997) describe the hallmarks that distinguish great teams (like Walt Disney's animators of Snow White and Lockheed Martin's Skunk Works and the Stealth Fighter) from so-so teams. They note that members of great groups are optimists, convinced they can do anything. The bottom line conclusion to be drawn from both is that great teams are composed of people who are optimistic in solving problems — problems that others frequently deem impossible. Doug Englebart, the founder of the Bootstrap Institute who was mentioned previously, emphasizes that achieving tomorrow's high-performance organizations will involve significant changes throughout their capability infra-structures. He believes that *groupware* will play a strategic role in this evolutionary strategy of our *augmentation system* (human and tool systems), and this infrastructure should be the obvious focus of attention in the quest for higher organizational performance. The idea is that over time our culture has evolved a rich system of things that when we are trained to use them, can *augment* our genetically endowed capabilities so that we and our organizations can exercise capabilities of a much higher nature than would be otherwise possible. The bottom line is that the complexity and urgency of the world's problems are increasing at a rate that is greater than humankind's ability to cope, challenging organizations to change in quantum leaps versus incremental steps. Human systems, specifically teams, have to evolve with tool systems in the era of the digital revolution, which can result in exponential increases in organizational collective IQ, in turn supercharging its ability to improve itself over time. This is where the real power of computers lie, not simply in automating our work processes, but in *augmenting human intellect* and ability to address the problems that some feel are reaching the point of no return, especially in the environmen-tal areas. Englebart believes that the formula for this type of organizational change must involve *CoDIAK* (Concurrent Development, Integration, and Application of Knowledge) capabilities. According to his model, most orga-nizations only operate on two dimensions — "*A*" *work*, or the development, support, and delivery of its essential product or service. This is the primary or core mission of the organization, like building cars or delivering health care. "*B*" *work*, or systems and activities, such as e-mail and quality management processes, are intended to improve the performance of "*A*" *work*. "*B*" *work* is likely to be basically the same among similar organiza-tions. "*B*" *work*, in a sense, is reducing product cycle time to make faster, smarter, higher quality "*A*" activities. Despite companies spending millions of dollars on such improvement processes, they seldom think about how to make the "*B*" *work* itself (the improvement processes) more effective. He then discusses the importance of "*C*" *work*, which is about improving the improvement process cycle time, to make faster, smarter, higher quality "*B*" activities. These are activities that boost the rate at which the improvement process can improve, from attending a TQM seminar to forming a consortium for enhancing an organization's *improvement infrastructure*. This whole process underscores the mandate for virtual and real-time, collaborative, team-based, networked improvement communities (NICs), and enterprise-wide knowledge management systems.

Finally, some generalized results from several primate studies indicate that a so-called *super group* of primates seem to have similar social group skills. This group tends to live longer than the rest, maintain higher status than their peers, and generally are a more successful lot. So what is their secret? First, they were good at threat assessment, they didn't waste energy and knew when to act. Second, they initiated response to threat and won 95 percent of the time (they knew when to act rather than get acted upon). Third, they knew clearly when they had won or lost and didn't fret over it but just moved on (every ape has his day). Fourth, they displaced frustration and were, hence, more calm and less reactive in their behavior. Finally, they were found to maintain a broad base of relationships within the social network. So, ape or human, good networking coupled with high EQ can be a key to success in the *jungle*.

More Bottom Line Recommendations:

- Good team skills will be requisite for the networked improvement communities (NICs) and collaborative communities of practice that will be more and more common in the era of the knowledge worker.
- Individually smart people can collectively do dumb things when part of a team. The whole is not the sum of the parts. Teams can be skewed towards a myopic like-mindedness and operate from an emotional and social blind side. Profiling team EQ can identify these situations. The choice then becomes either trying to increase the skills of the team in the area of the blind side to offset the skew or importing other members with these skills to offset the blind side.
- Conversely, consider EQ profiles when assembling high-performance teams to achieve the creative tension necessary to offset the EQ blind-side effect.
- There is no substitute for a broad base of social relationships in getting things done in the team-based networked environment that characterizes today's corporate environment.

- Knowledge management and groupware systems support and augment the capabilities of high-performance teams.
- The most important "C" activity for organizations is to encourage and fund cross-functional improvement communities tasked with working on common challenges to improve the improvement process. Additionally, we need to get better at scanning the future competitive environment and establishing the right pilots to exploit return on investment, strategic first strike advantage, and improvement cycle times (an improvement process "skunkworks" if you will).

Two other factors of emotional and social intelligence that can make a big difference are optimism and trust, which will be discussed in detail below.

Optimism:

Optimism is a very important EQ factor and one of the most important for overall success in life and, particularly, in the workplace. Based on our research findings, optimism has been shown to be one of the strongest predictors of success and retention in a marketing and sales environment. It seems that it is especially helpful in maintaining confidence in dealing with the adversity of rejection characteristically associated with the sales environment. Otherwise, it seems to be a sheer force of will that has a powerful effect in succeeding in the face of failure. Consider that in the process of inventing the light bulb in 1879, Thomas Edison tried and failed more than 1,000 times. When asked if he had ever become discouraged, Edison reportedly answered:

Those were steps on the way. In each attempt I was successful in finding a way not to create a light bulb. I was always eager to learn, even from my mistakes.

Trust:

Individuals high in emotional and social intelligence are able to display the character needed to promote trust in their coworkers. They do this through maintaining a consistency between their actions and words. High levels of trust also seem to improve problem solving, interpersonal cooperation, and tend to reduce stress. Also, it is the foundation upon which all close personal relationships must rest. Lack of trust is a tremendous depleter of time and resources in the organization. Just imagine how much cost is associated with the time we spend in checking on others and protecting ourselves from possible threats from those we don't trust. Military studies have shown that units with high degrees of group cohesiveness, confidence, and trust have dealt better with the rigors of combat. These units have experienced far fewer combat stress casualties (i.e., being incapacitated by anxiety and fear), primarily due to this self-others integration. Individuals were able to focus on the mission at hand versus watching their back and were willing to risk their life if necessary for their buddies, because they knew that their buddies would do the same for them. Leadership trust and confidence has also been shown to be a factor in this area as well. Trusting that the leader will commit the team to missions commensurate with their skills is decisive and will help the team make the right decisions under fire.

In addition to our work and that of others who have employed the Bar-On model and test (the EQ-i) of emotional and social intelligence, the foregoing suggestions for understanding and improving personal and organizational effectiveness are based on a wide variety of research findings from a number of sources. For example, we will compare, from time to time, our findings and suggestions with those of the United States Office of Personnel Management (OPM). The OPM has conducted very serious research for nearly half a century in the area of management; they have identified twenty-two key managerial competencies recommended to be used "in developing selection criteria, performance standards, and training curricula" (Corts & Gowing, 1992; Gregory & Park, 1992).

The Outline of This Book and How to Make the Best Use of It for Improving Organizational Effectiveness

The next five chapters of this book provide the reader with a clear and comprehensive road map for understanding the importance of the fifteen factorial components of emotional and social intelligence and how best to improve them in order to improve organizational effectiveness. These five chapters divide the fifteen key factors of emotional and social intelligence into the five major components of this concept: intrapersonal capacity, interpersonal skills, adaptability, stress management, and general mood. The reader can either browse through these chapters stopping to zero in on those factors that interest them most or systematically review all of these factors, one after the other, to best understand the entirety of this very important concept and how it will impact your organization's bottom line. For each of the fifteen emotional and social skills discussed, the reader is first presented with a definition of that factor, and then shown how it is related to organizational performance; this is followed by a SWOT analysis (clearly describing the potential strengths, weaknesses, opportunities, and threats for the organization associated with high and low levels of the factor involved), and finally the reader is presented with numerous ways of individually and organizationally improving the factor under discussion. Additional hints to improving corporate EQ and functioning are offered in the Afterword and in the Appendix.

PART 1:
Intrapersonal Capacity

Intrapersonal capacity describes the inner self. The factors included in this domain are *self-regard, emotional self-awareness, assertiveness, independence*, and *self-actualization*. Enhanced intrapersonal capacity indicate individuals who know themselves, feel good about themselves, are in touch with their feelings, and feel positive about what they are doing in their lives. These people are able to express their feelings, and they are independent, strong, and confident in conveying their feelings, ideas, and beliefs. Our research findings have revealed that a well-developed intrapersonal capacity is very important for senior managers, marketing professionals, teachers, psychologists, and psychiatrists.

Self-Regard

Self-regard is the ability to be aware of, understand, accept, and respect oneself. To be aware of and understand oneself means knowing who one is and understanding why one thinks, feels, and behaves the way one does. Accurate self-assessment depends upon efficient self-awareness. Respecting oneself, essentially, is liking the way one is. Self-acceptance is the ability to accept one's perceived positive and negative aspects as well as one's limitations and possibilities. This conceptual component of emotional, personal, and social intelligence is associated with general feelings of security, inner strength, self-assuredness, self-confidence, and feelings of self-adequacy. Feeling sure of oneself is dependent upon self-respect and self-esteem, which are based on a fairly well-developed sense of identity. A person with positive self-regard feels fulfilled and satisfied with himself or herself. At the opposite end of the continuum are feelings of personal inadequacy and inferiority. Self-awareness and accurate self-assessment together with self-confidence are considered to be important managerial competencies.

Strengths Associated with High Levels of Self-Regard:

Individuals with high levels of self-regard tend to accept and respect themselves and have positive self-esteem. These people have a strong sense of self and self-identity; they know who they are and feel positive about themselves. They typically feel fulfilled and satisfied with themselves. To have strength in the area of self-regard is critical to many jobs. Positive self-regard is especially important for those working in management, sales, marketing, and teaching.

This strength is also based on awareness of one's shortcomings, with a knowledge of how to compensate for these shortcomings. Positive self-regard is, thus, tempered with humility. Andy Grove, who helped found Intel Corporation, is credited with saying that only the paranoid survive and authored a book by the same name (*Only the Paranoid Survive: How to Exploit the Crisis Points That Challenge Every Company and Career*). His point is that the time to be paranoid is when you are successful or feeling too self-content. The idea is that we have to avoid the *inertia of success*. In this light, we have to avoid falling into the trap of believing that we are so competent, that everything is going so well, and that nothing bad will happen. Business success is transitory, and businesses usually fail because they became dependent upon the same strategic and tactical moves that previously worked for them, got mired in the inertia of success, and were surprised by change to which management could not adapt. Grove notes that change approaches quietly *on cat's feet* and that it's essential to understand *strategic inflection points* to avoid being caught off guard. Grove notes that these strategic inflection points can mean opportunity, or signal the coming of the end. He cites an example from his own career that points to the importance of admitting a shortcoming and that we need to learn. The more successful we are, the harder it tends to be to make that admission. If we don't fight this tendency, this very success can become a wall that isolates us from learning new things to compensate for our short-comings and can be the strategic inflection point that spells opportunity or decline, based on how we handle it. Grove notes that when Intel was trans-forming itself from a maker of mainframe computers to one that would play a central role in the personal computer industry, he realized that he needed to learn more about the software side of the industry. He swallowed his pride, admitted he knew little about this business, and deliberately started spending time with software people, taking notes and literally going back to school. This exemplifies the way self-regard is defined in the Bar-On model. This is awareness of strengths tempered with a *healthy paranoia* to avoid the inertia of success, listening for the cat's feet of strategic inflection points and learning to change and admit when we need to learn new skills. The bottom line is that we need to avoid being a legend in our own mind, lest we get lulled to sleep by our own virtues and fail to see that the emperor is wearing no clothes.

Weaknesses Associated with Low Levels of Self-Regard:

If self-regard is underdeveloped and weak, this typically indicates low self-esteem, feelings of low self-worth, negative or pessimistic attitudes towards self and weaknesses in the areas of confidence, security, and adequacy. It also can imply a lack of inner strength and a poor sense of self-identity, perhaps bordering on deep feelings of inadequacy and inferiority. In the more extreme conditions, this can lead to self-hatred and feelings of hopelessness and fearfulness.

From a corporate perspective, it typically can indicate a culture of defeat and despair, poor morale, lack of *esprit de corps*, and potentially a lack of group cohesiveness. Many of the maladaptive defense patterns one sees in the workplace typically serve the purpose of protection from the pain of low self-esteem. In studies conducted with adults in treatment and prison as well as with juveniles in detention, the lack of social problem-solving skills appears to coexist with low self-esteem. Individuals who believe in their own personal resources are far better suited to live life successfully than those who are paralyzed by self-doubt and self-distrust. The individual with little or no confidence in his or her ability often allows someone else to run his or her life. How often does something positive come from that? In the workplace, individuals with a clear sense of their own value tend to treat others well, since they expect that others are going to deal with them in the same way. They typically don't tolerate mistreatment and have the assertiveness to confront the behavior or find another relationship in which they will be treated better. In general, when self-esteem is threatened by some comment or remark (regardless of the intentions), the response typically is defense and emotionally based rather than one geared to deal with the situation in a rational manner. For the majority of individuals who work for a living, the job is a central element to their self-esteem. Work tends to influence and contribute to one's self-concept, and workers tend to develop a sense of their competence and mastery over themselves and their environment. Additionally, the job gives workers day-in and day-out the message that they have something to offer — they are engaging in activities that produce something valued by others. For individuals or companies plagued by poor self-regard, the focus tends to be that they are not making the grade. Since we invoke defense mechanisms to avoid reduction of self-evaluation and the accompanying sense of failure, this message can ultimately create an emotional virus that compromises positive emotional health and corporate performance.

Potential Opportunities Associated with Average Levels of Self-Regard:

Ever since the 1890s when William James proposed the theory that self-concept is acquired through human interaction rather than being an inborn character trait, a great deal of research has been devoted to how self-concept and self-esteem develop. The opportunity to improve self-regard on a personal level has to begin with the realization that self-regard is generated from within. Nathaniel Branden, a clinical psychologist and author of *Six Pillars of Self-Esteem*, notes that self-esteem is aided when individuals are treated with respect and are inspired rather than being the object of a demand. On a corporate level, in addition to the obvious need to treat people with respect and acceptance, is the need to allow for learning. It is important to allow workers to struggle a bit with the challenge of solving problems rather than stepping in and doing it for them. Workers need to know the extent of their own abilities and that they can overcome problems even if it takes a certain amount of time and effort. In this regard, one of the most important tasks in workforce development in this area is teaching employees how to think versus what to think. Critical thinking is an important bridge between the affective and cognitive world of self to practical application of skills in solving interpersonal problems to solving problems at work. Here the idea is to teach employees in such a way that encourages the development and encouragement of thinking — giving them the intellectual skills they need to learn and make use of the information. Lest we think that these skills are already taught by schools, John Goodland noted in *A Place Called School* that in observing over 1,000 classrooms, he found less than 1 percent of *teacher talk* encouraged or elicited open student response, such as offering an opinion or supporting it with evidence. The role of the family is also central to self-esteem. Research has indicated that the central component in effective coping with life stress appeared to be constant feedback from a few adults early in life. An assumption within the prevention arena has been that increasing individual's social problem-solving skills will improve their ability to communicate with others and, thereby, reduce a series of undesirable behaviors that detract not only from their self-esteem but from their ability to acquire the skills necessary to increase their sense of personal control and enhance self-regard.

Threats Associated with Very Low Levels of Self-Regard:

From the above, it becomes abundantly clear that leaders must possess considerable interpersonal skills to deal with employees on work-related matters in order to avoid acting in a manner so as to threaten an employee's self-esteem and set off a defensive trip wire. While defense mechanisms serve to protect employee self-regard, they typically do little to produce positive solutions to the problems at hand. The point is that rather than lower their self-evaluation to match their purported performance, employees typically dispose of negative views of their performance through defense mechanisms. Unless leaders handle these situations properly, they will fail to achieve the almost universal management objective of improving the employee's performance. The skill of protecting employee self-esteem and at the same time accomplishing the business objective is a learned skill that requires training. Low self-regard can play out in the powerful concept of the self-fulfilling prophecy, whether it be on an individual or organizational level. The bottom line is that we are what we think, so low self-regard can have the negative influence of trapping individuals and entire groups of personnel at levels beneath their true capability. The ultimate threat is the infectious defeat and despair that seem to be the running mates of poor self-regard, that can contribute to a performance death spiral that becomes difficult to recover from.

Bottom Line Suggestions for Improving Self-Regard

"Personal Remedies":

- List the positive and negative feelings you have about yourself, and see how those feelings affect you.
- Reevaluate the way you have been thinking about yourself up till now.
- Think of ways you can actively change and improve the way you think about yourself.
- Purposely reexamine the negative thoughts you have about yourself, and ask yourself a few basic questions: when did they first begin, how, and why; were these negative thoughts about yourself originally your own thoughts or someone else's; were or are these thoughts really correct, and are they really applicable to you today; and how do you think you would feel if you didn't think that way about yourself.
- Avoid comparing yourself to others.
- Think of how you can improve your negative points (if they are really negative).

- List some of the negative thoughts you have of yourself, and then try to reverse those thoughts 180 degrees to positive ones and see how it makes you fell.
- Purposely STOP thinking negatively about yourself, and begin to think more positively about yourself.
- List your strengths, positive attributes, and accomplishments that you are proud of, reflect on them, and make a point of celebrating these points.
- Be more proud of your accomplishments, and tell others about them.

"Group Remedies":

- Provide immediate positive feedback for efficient group performance and accomplishments whenever possible.
- Go out of your way to make subordinates and coworkers feel good about their work and themselves.
- Make them feel appreciated.
- Encourage subordinates and coworkers to take personal pride in their work and in the contributions that they are making.
- When giving negative feedback, do it a constructive and matter-of-fact manner — don't turn it into an attack on the person's ego.
- Organize a group at work, or perhaps a retreat, in which you can discuss the group weaknesses and work on how to improve the areas that need to be improved.
- Explain what is meant by self-regard and how it's important for one's overall ability to successfully cope with daily demand.
- Emphasize why improving this skill will have an overall positive effect on the effectiveness and productivity of the organization as a whole.
- Link the importance of knowing oneself better to getting along better with others and being more successful and productive at work.
- Ask them to tell each other all the good things they are doing at work and at home.
- Encourage them to discuss various ways they can change the negative thinking that they have about themselves.

Emotional Self-Awareness

Emotional self-awareness is the ability to recognize and understand one's feelings. It is not only the ability to be aware of one's feelings and emotions, but also to differentiate between them, to know what one is feeling and why, and to know what caused those feelings. Being aware of emotions is highly associated with the ability and willingness to share those emotions with others. Being aware of internal states is a prerequisite to be in control of one's emotions and is thought to be an important managerial competency

Self-awareness begins with the ability to recognize one's feelings and describe them. This is critical to later being able to see the links between our thoughts, feelings, and reactions and to know what's driving what. Is my decision being influenced by an emotion, such as anger, and if so, how likely is it to be a wise decision when it is driven by this emotion? To not be able to identify these internal feeling states, and differentiate between them, tends to lead to behavior that is emotionally fused, which has its obvious consequences. Another aspect of emotional self-awareness that is connected with self-regard is the awareness of your emotional strengths and weaknesses, which influences your ability to see yourself in a positive light, but tempered with reality. Additionally, self-awareness also relates to empathy. How can we be successful in identifying and reading the emotions of others (empathy) when we are unable to identify or are out of touch with our own?

Emotional self-awareness is one thing, and being able to do express emotions and have control over them is another. Many of us are able to identify that we are mad or angry, but frequently excuse our wrong behavior as a result of this anger by such classics as "they made me do it" or "they made me mad." Nonsense! We choose to feel the way we feel and to react the way we do. Nothing can have that kind of power over us unless we choose to let it. Aha, but there's the rub. This would mean that we have to actually take responsibility for our reactions, feelings, and behavior versus so handily being able to use such responsibility avoiding tactics as projection, denial, rationalization, and avoidance. Albert Ellis, father of *rational emotive therapy*, has a good model that focuses on awareness of what we tell ourselves consciously or unconsciously about the events in our lives and our reactions to them. Ellis believes that the result of this process is often irrational beliefs. The Ellis model involves the "ABCD" process:

A. **Identify the activating event** — This is the specific event or situation that preceded our current distress, such as an argument with your spouse or a conflict at work.

B. **Examine your belief** (often irrational) about the event — What is it you tell yourself about this event? What does it mean to you? Many times, these beliefs pass through the filters of shoulds and musts ("My boss should appreciate my work" and "Others must do as I say"). This usually results in the follow-on irrational processes of awfulizing or blowing events out of proportion ("Since they don't like me, it's absolutely awful") and low frustration tolerance, which is viewing frustration and discomfort as intolerable rather than inconvenient ("Since I can't have my way, it is intolerable").

C. **Consider the consequences of your irrational thinking** — The more you are aware of your irrational beliefs, the easier it will be for you to free yourself from emotionally fused undesirable emotional and behavioral consequences. This step is, in a sense, a cause-and-effect analysis. This is exemplified by "since life should not include challenges, and mine does, then it is awful." Therefore, "I'm likely to spend a lot of time and energy feeling resentful, discouraged, depressed," and so forth. Also, "since I can't control what happens to me, it's not my fault, nor my responsibility." "I guess I'm just a hapless victim...it always rains on me!"

Accept the fact that life is not fair. When you realize that it may be difficult at times, but it's not awful and therefore not impossible, you can begin to focus on taking responsibility and working on the main issues at hand.

D. **Dispute your irrational beliefs** — Simply doing ABC isn't enough. You must aggressively and vigorously challenge and dispute these irrational and ineffective beliefs and self-talk. Some ways to dispute irrational beliefs are as follows:

   1. **Evidence** — "Where is the evidence to prove that I should always get what I want?" "Where is it written?"

2. **Logic** — "Where is the logic, and how does it follow that I must be good at everything I do?"
3. **Pragmatism** — "Is this belief really helping me achieve my goals?" "Would a different belief be more helpful?"
4. **Role-playing** — Have a friend or spouse repeat your irrational beliefs one at a time while you forcefully argue against them.

Strengths Associated with High Levels of Emotional Self-Awareness:

High levels of emotional self-awareness indicate individuals who are in touch with their feelings and emotions; they know what they are feeling and understand why they feel the way that they do. Well-developed emotional self-awareness is critical for being empathetic, which is the ability to read the emotions of others. If one can't identify and differentiate between their own emotions, how effective can they skillfully read the emotions of others? High levels of self-awareness are dependent upon knowing *what* one is feeling and *why*. Through the ages, this type of self-awareness has been touted as a requisite for true wisdom. Indeed, this skill is critically associated with wisely choosing responses to others and situations, versus being emotionally out of control in response to these situations (*emotionally hijacked*). This is also an essential skill in strategic decision making. It is important to be aware of the emotional tenor within oneself and within the organization as a prerequisite to knowing when to displace frustration or bind anxiety, when it's wise to avoid making a decision, and when it's time to act. Good emotional self-awareness is a key component in intuitive reasoning. It's knowing oneself and the organization to the point of knowing when to listen to that still small voice within us and act intuitively, and when not to. Well-developed emotional self-awareness has been demonstrated as an important and valuable emotional skill in professions like clinical psychology, psychiatry, and social work.

Weaknesses Associated with Low Levels of Emotional Self-Awareness:

Some people who are deficient in emotional self-awareness describe themselves as feeling numb or empty. Serious deficiencies in this area are found in alexithymic conditions (the inability to describe and express feelings verbally), which are often associated with psychosomatic disorders.

Underdeveloped emotional self-awareness tends to undermine the effectiveness of several other emotional and social skills. As previously discussed, empathy, or the ability to read the emotions of others, is definitely compromised. Furthermore, it renders us susceptible to acting on impulse under the heat of an emotion like anger, since we are not aware that we were angry in the first place. Moreover, flexibility could be attenuated since this involves the ability to *adjust* one's emotions, feelings, and behaviors to changing situations and conditions. Foundational to this emotional self-awareness is the ability to monitor oneself in relation to the external environment, to know when we are out of sync, and when it's time to adjust. Very closely related to this skill is reality testing, the ability to assess correspondence between what is experienced (what you tell yourself about a situation), and what objectively exists.

Being emotionally unaware tends to lead us towards being emotionally hijacked or fused in our response to reality, since we tend to act based on emotional bleedover into our cognitive thought processes. Because I'm angry, I interpret a request from my boss to speed up my work as a threat, so I then respond with passive aggression by deliberately slowing down even more. However, an important reality test in this situation would be to ask "Who said that having the boss demand that I speed up my work is a threat?"

Potential Opportunities Associated with Average Levels of Emotional Self-Awareness:

The opportunities to improve in emotional self-awareness are many. As discussed previously, it must begin with learning to be aware of the influence of our own perceptions. One of the most rudimentary approaches that has been popular in schools that teach emotional literacy is the "stoplight" approach. This approach encourages children to see the *red light*, stop, calm down, gain perspective, and think before acting when they are aware of feeling upset. The *yellow light* is designed to encourage a cause-and-effect analysis, which means to think about the things you might do while upset and the consequences of each possible action. The *green light* part of this approach means to pick the best course of action and try it out. Besides helping with impulse control, this activity helps in making the distinction between having the feeling, and what you do with it and how you act when you feel that way. Other popular names for this type of approach are "take time out," "hit the pause button," and "stop the video." This technique is widely used in anger management training for adults as well, and it focuses on *the critical first step* of learning to identify the feeling state that should prompt appropriate and efficient emotional regulation. Before this skill is adequately mastered, it's okay for the parent, teacher, spouse, friend, coworker or boss engaged with the person to say "I think we need to take time out." The rules are to physically separate from each other and allow time for emotions to subside and reason to have a chance to take hold. After a period of time, the discussion can be continued, hopefully, in a more thoughtful, less emotionally charged manner. In these "time out" periods, one cannot pursue the other and continue with the discussion. Some approaches suggest going out and taking a walk or doing some other form of physical activity. To avoid using this technique as a convenient "cop out" when one doesn't want to deal with someone, the old saying of "don't let the sun set on your anger" might help. Try not to allow twenty-four hours to pass after a time out before re-engaging the issue. The bottom line is that feelings have a major influence on our decisions, and when we make decisions, the brain just doesn't automatically do a cause-and-effect analysis. Instead, it tends to work by a more "sloppy logic," quickly sizing up situations, making some gross analogies to past experience in your cognitive repertoire, then producing a feeling about what you should do. When we are emotionally self-aware, this tends to be shaped by reason of our entire life wisdom and experience. When we aren't in touch with our feelings, we tend not to hear the still small voice of reason and what we should do. The above mentioned tactics not only contribute to good impulse control and responsible behavior, but they also increase emotional self-awareness in the process.

Make a daily habit of concentrating as much as possible on emotional self-awareness, listening to yourself, and observing your behavior. Some have even found it helpful to rate how they feel in general on a scale from 1 to 10 and then to break that down into various feelings like happiness, sadness, anger, and so forth. This strategy can even be used in the workplace with coworkers when and where it is appropriate. For the person chairing a meeting to say that he or she feels like a "2" today may have some interesting implications for the process and the outcome of that meeting! When we are able "to take an emotional temperature," we are able to calm ourselves when feeling anxious, cheer ourselves up when feeling down, or appropriately express anger when feeling upset. Such activities like exercise, meditation, relaxation, listening to music, or being involved in hobbies tend to help. Herbert Benson, author of *The Relaxation Response* and *The Wellness Book: The Comprehensive Guide To Maintaining Health and Treating Stress-Related Illness*, suggests a basic relaxation technique that has been widely used since his first book was printed in 1975:

- Sit comfortably with your eyes closed.
- Breath deeply from the stomach — some have found it helpful to place their hand on their abdomen to feel their hand gently rise.
- Silently repeat the word one as you exhale or just focus on your breathing. A modification to this is to focus on a pleasurable memory as you do this. We all have those thoughts of a certain place, person, or experience that evoke positive feelings. Some have even found it helpful to do this while listening to soothing music. If you have any intrusive thoughts, just continue the deep breathing.

Studies have shown that if this exercise is practiced ten to twenty minutes daily, people generally feel calmer and are better able to deal with everyday problems. It has also been found to be beneficial for people who suffer from high blood pressure, chronic pain, and insomnia.

The following technique can be used as soon as we are aware that we're getting upset, tense, anxious, or angry:

- Breath deeply to interrupt the thought related to your present feelings.
- Identify the negative and illogical aspects these feelings, and challenge them with evidence to the contrary using Ellis' ABCD model, which was previously mentioned.

Humor also has a powerful effect on changing emotional states and can transform even the most upsetting situations. Norman Cousins stressed the value of laughter in inducing positive emotions as a tool in dealing with his own illness in *Anatomy of an Illness*. He discovered this primarily through watching humorous videos. This was later researched at Loma Linda University, where the researchers found lowered levels of cortisol and adrenaline in the bloodstream. These substances are produced by the body in times of stress and are thought to suppress general immunity.

As previously mentioned, physical exercise can play a powerful role in helping us become more aware of our bodies and internal feelings as well as deal with our moods. Aerobic exercise produces endorphins, natural chemicals in the brain that affect mood and tend to act as a natural antidepressant. Even mild aerobic activity of at least twenty minutes in duration, such as a brisk walk, can be beneficial in mood management. An added bonus is that just exposing oneself to sunlight can act as another natural antidepressant, and many find a positive benefit of spending time in a natural setting. The key to exercise for mood management is consistency. It seems to supply a steady stream of endorphins, which could actually help protect one from depressive moods. There are many other strategies that aid in emotional self-awareness and mood regulation that have been employed for many years.

Threats Associated with Very Low Levels of Emotional Self-Awareness:

When looking at potential threats, the question to be addressed is what other emotional and social deficits combine with deficits in emotional self-awareness to pose the greatest danger to an individual or organization. First of all, deficits in emotional self-awareness can seriously limit one's ability to be empathetic as was previously mentioned. It is logical to assume that if one has difficulty in recognizing and understanding one's own emotions, he or she will not be that successful in tuning into and accurately reading other's emotions. Secondly, when one is unaware of one's own emotions, there is at times a bleedover effect with reality testing. It is obvious that our emotions can have an ill effect on our ability to view situations realistically; and such perception is complicated even more so if one is not that aware of one's own emotions. Moreover, underdeveloped emotional self-awareness, lack of empathy, and poor reality testing make it nearly impossible to succeed in interpersonal relationships. Finally, another skill that seems to be affected by low levels of emotional self-awareness is flexibility (the ability to adjust one's emotions to changing situations). Once again, the obvious question is, "How successful can I really be in adjusting my emotions to changing situations when I'm not that aware of my emotions?" To exemplify the problematics involved, let's say that when I perceive that I am being criticized, I feel they are really telling me that I am stupid, which makes me angry. I can't determine when I'm getting angry, it just happens, and before I know it, I am in a fit of rage. Since I am not good at being aware of such emotions, how flexible can I be in learning to adjust to constructive feedback from a friend? Perhaps the only way I know is to tell that person: "Just don't criticize me." Perhaps, just perhaps, it is I who has to adjust and be more flexible in my acceptance and response to feedback — after all, who says that feedback means "I'm stupid"? It is obvious that "I need skill in gauging and monitoring my emotions so that I can adjust to different situations." What would happen if my boss tries to give me feedback? What happens if I blow up at him or her? Do I say, "Just don't criticize me, and this won't happen." Sadly, this scenario happens all too often, leading some people through a litany of failed relationships and multiple jobs that all just mysteriously "blew up" in their face.

Care must be taken not to speculate too much about threats from skill-set deficits, because people and organizations are different and frequently learn to compensate to offset these deficits. The point the authors want to make is that certain emotional and social skill deficits have an attenuating, bleedover effect on other skills, which creates a sense of built-in drag and inertia we must overcome to compensate. The best approach is to work to improve skills that are weak and underdeveloped in order to decrease drag and lighten our load!

Bottom Line Suggestions for Improving Emotional Self-Awareness

"Personal Remedies":

- Make a conscious effort to better understand the way you feel as the first step to controlling and expressing those feelings and better understanding the way other people feel.

- Don't get swept away with your emotions or try to avoid them, but make an effort to stay with those feelings and understand them.
- Try not to be embarrassed about the way you feel — this is an important part of being alive and being human.
- Learn to be more aware of the way you feel in general, and to know more accurately how you're feeling at any give time and why.
- Keep track of certain situations, record how you generally feel in these situations, and try to understand why.
- If you feel very emotional about something, try to understand what exactly you are feeling and why (love, hate, fear, excitement, and so forth.).
- When you are angry, try to understand exactly how you feel and what made you feel that way.
- Try to improve your ability to accurately differentiate between similar types of emotions like annoyance, anxiety, and fear.
- Try to clarify similar types of feelings like being bored or being sad, liking or loving a person, hating or fearing someone or something, and so forth.
- Consider whether a surface feeling may be caused by some underlying deeper feeling. For example, experiences of anger happening at the surface level may really be the result of deeper feelings of fear, frustration, and disappointment, which may still remain after the anger disappears.

"Group Remedies":

- Provide the means whereby people at work can share and discuss their feelings.
- Try to encourage subordinates and coworkers to look more deeply at themselves.
- Ask the people you work with how they're feeling more often.
- If you see that someone is having a good day and looks happy, ask him/her how they feel.
- If someone appears confused, lost or frustrated, ask what's happening.
- If someone looks angry, ask what's happening with him/her.
- Try to organize a group at work, or perhaps a retreat, in which you

can discuss emotional self-awareness and how to improve this emotional skill.

- Explain what is meant by emotional self-awareness and how it's important for one's overall ability to successfully cope with daily demand.
- Emphasize why improving this skill will have an overall positive effect on the productivity of the organization as a whole.
- Have them start talking about the lighter feelings like liking things, happiness, being pleasantly surprised, and satisfaction and what brings them to smile and laugh.
- Move on to discussions of stronger emotions like what makes them bored, edgy, annoyed, frustrated, sad, angry — and how much they are aware of these feelings.

Assertiveness

Assertiveness is the ability to express feelings, beliefs, and thoughts and to defend one's rights in a nondestructive manner. Assertiveness is composed of three basic components: (1) the ability to express feelings (i.e., to accept and express anger, warmth, and other emotions), (2) the ability to express beliefs and thoughts openly (i.e., to voice opinions, disagree, and take a definite stand), and (3) the ability to stand up for personal rights (i.e., not to allow others to bother you or take advantage of you). Assertive people are able to express their feelings and affirm themselves, are guided by their principles, can stand up for their rights, and take care of themselves. They are not overly controlled or shy — they are able to outwardly express their feelings (often discretely), without being aggressive or abusive. To adequately assert oneself is a prerequisite to effective communication and is an important factor in being decisive; these are considered to be important managerial competencies based on research conducted by the US Office of Personnel Management (Corts & Gowing, 1992). Not only is this attribute vital for managers, but it is very important for sales people, insurance agents, and especially for individuals working in marketing based on our research.

This domain of emotional intelligence is about degree and balance. Having the right amount of assertiveness without being aggressive or abusive versus being shy and nonassertive. It involves a certain amount of self-confidence and positive self-regard, to the extent that seeking approval at the cost of standing up for rights will not be compromised. Some tend to struggle with the tendency to become abusive or aggressive when in these situations. This emotional skill also requires a certain degree of three other emotional and social skills: emotional self-awareness, empathy, and impulse control. In order to avoid being abusive and aggressive, we first have to have adequate emotional self-awareness to realize when we are getting angry, then good impulse control to keep us from acting on our impulses, and finally fairly well-developed empathy to accurately read and respect the feelings and concerns of others. For example, say we are feeling somewhat angry at being confronted by the boss for a mistake we made, we need adequately developed emotional self-awareness to identify the onset of this feeling, which may stem, for instance, from a deeper feeling of inadequacy that surfaces when we make mistakes. Since we are aware of this, we are better able to deal with the underlying stress and control the impulse allowing the boss to give feedback, especially, if we are able to accurately read the situation as a nonthreatening coaching session.

Strengths Associated with High Levels of Assertiveness:

High levels of assertiveness indicate people who are able to express feelings, thoughts, and beliefs and defend their rights in a nondestructive manner; these people are rarely limited by uncomfortable feelings of self-consciousness or bashfulness. They are often described as bold. Based on our research findings, assertiveness is a key factor for being successful in various occupations like sales, marketing, and management.

When this particular skill is assessed as a strength in a person or organization, it will almost always involve the aforementioned emotional and social skills to keep it in balance, especially good impulse control and empathy as well as a knowledge of when, how, and to what degree assertiveness can be applied to the situation at hand. Assertiveness and the ability to listen are very important components in interpersonal communication. Efficient communication is not only dependent upon our ability to express ourselves, but is also dependent upon well-developed emotional self-awareness (listening to ourselves), empathy (listening to others), positive interpersonal relationship (establishing a constructive framework in which dialogue takes place), reality testing (accurately sizing up what is being expressed), flexibility (being tolerant of others and able to alter our views), stress tolerance, and impulse control (adequately managing emotions in order to prevent them from interfering with what is being expressed). Within this context, an old saying exemplifies one important aspect of assertiveness: "if you aim at nothing, you'll hit it every time." If we don't know what we want or what we are aiming for, we shouldn't be surprised when we don't get it. The reason why many people don't get what they want is because of lack of assertiveness. The idea conveyed here is that clarity of purpose as to our destination, together with a well-developed ability to communicate, which depends on a high level of assertiveness, facilitates our ability to achieve what we want to achieve. Assertive people have learned to be specific in asking for what they want, communicate precisely, and read others as they are communicating — making the right adjustments literally on the fly. Once again, this means using empathy to generate trust, comfort, and a feeling of similarity between self and others. Empathy is helpful in understanding others and emotionally reading the situation. This involves tuning in, listening, and paying close attention to what others are saying; it means assessing verbal and nonverbal behavior as well as listening to the tempo of speech and tone of voice. Empathy is an extremely important communication skill that involves observing both content and style in order to understand what is important to others, what they care about, and what they want. Asserting one's ideas and views within the context of interpersonal communication is strongly dependent upon input from this type of tuning into others (empathy), as well as to tuning into oneself (emotional self-awareness).

Anthony Robbins and Joseph McClendon created a communication technique called "mirroring" (*Bottom Line/Personal*, April 15, 1997). They suggest paying close attention to the people with whom you are speaking and then finding something in common with them by *mirroring* them. Mirroring is done by matching your gestures to theirs, which includes content and style of speech, tempo, inflection, choice of words, and body movements. This doesn't mean you're merely mimicking or copying them. On the contrary, mirroring is designed to communicate that you're in tune with them; it, thus, builds rapport and overcomes differences that often create distance. Once in sync, the object is to lead the conversation in the direction that you want it to go. People who are assertive and empathic are typically able to do this quite easily. They seem to be able to connect with others immediately, facilitate people, and easily interact with them. This type of communication involves accurate reading of social cues to determine the right angle of attack, rapid processing of information, and thinking quickly on you feet to make the appropriate on-the-fly adjustments. This often includes the art of structuring win-win proposi-tions where possible to facilitate the whole process. It is important to make use of as much information as possible from this type of interpersonal interaction (language, gestures, meaning, and belief systems) in order to communicate personally with the person in support of the process of facil-itative conditioning. Several examples support this point. The first example is based on one of the authors' experience as a consultant to a senior manager in a session with the VP of a large firm. The VP was a large, imposing man with a gruff demeanor and a reputation for "shooting the messenger." The VP would not sign and implement a proposed company-wide HR initiative, aimed at human behavior risk reduction. In a sense, he was playing devil's advocate and roughing up the hapless manager in the process. When the author was finally asked by the VP his opinion, it was a classic *act or get acted upon* scenario. The goal was clear: salvage the proposal, transact business with the VP, and get the signature, and allow the VP to take something away from the process as well. During the discussion between the VP and the Manager, the author had scanned the room, the VP's desk, his tone of voice, accent, and so forth. The idea was to somehow use these artifacts to connect personally with the VP, literally on the spot. The seeming right angle came through the VP's trying to use a line from his favorite movie, "What we have here is a failure to communicate," the title of which neither he nor the manager could remember (*Cool Hand Luke,* starring Paul Newman). At that opportune time, the author cited the movie title and star, which pleased the VP. Noticing previously the VP's southern drawl, and noting a coaster on his desk from a southern university, the author gambled and used these artifacts to leverage this angle of attack in response to the VP. The author in a self-effacing manner, looking the VP in the eyes as he spoke, noted that he was looking at this problem perhaps much more simply than the VP and the manager, this down-to-earth analysis style being largely due his rural family upbringing in the south. The author then paused, waiting for his guess as to the angle of potential cultural similarity (based upon the observed artifacts) to either hit or miss. The VP leaned forward abruptly in an almost conciliatory response to the author's self-effacing comments, noting that there was nothing wrong with that analysis style, since he himself had similar upbringing. He went on to note that he indeed went to the university on his desk, and that he was planning on retiring in the author's home state, and did the author know the area? The author noted he did, and the VP literally pulled a map out of his drawer, slid close to the author, and showed him his plot of land. From that, he returned to the business at hand, noting he would sign off on the initiative, and there was no need to even run it by the CEO, he would take care of that himself. On the way out, the manager noted her thanks for getting her out of the jam, especially "when he had me on that movie title." The point of this example is that in being successfully assertive in transacting your business and in a sense getting what you need, much of the outcome is in the strategy of the *angle of attack*. Some of that can be thought out and planned ahead of time, but some is literally on the spot and involves thinking on your feet. A second example (though the verbal response is not admirable) is from the classic Dr. Seuss movie, *How the Grinch Stole Christmas*. There is a scene in which the Grinch, dressed up like Santa Claus, is stealing all the Christmas "stuff" from the Whos. In the scene, the Grinch is stealing the tree. Little Cindy Lou Who wakes up, sees him, and questions "Santa" as to what he's doing. Seemingly dead in the water, the Grinch was shedding great drops of sweat. But, in classic quick thinking on your feet and using the artifacts at hand (the Christmas tree he was taking, his being dressed like Santa, and Cindy Lou Who thinking he was Santa), the Grinch responded. The narrator noted that the old Grinch "thought up a lie and he thought it up quick". . . noting that "Santa" noticed a light out on the tree and was merely taking it back to his shop to fix it. With that, he got her a drink of water and put her to bed. Though telling a lie is not admirable, the example is about using the artifacts of the situation, which the Grinch made good use of. An old Washington insider who had served in two different presidential administrations, told one of the authors, "It's a matter of getting good at your ABC's"...*alliance* building, *bargaining* (collecting chips), and *compromise*. The wisdom of this logic is clear: long-term success and survival is about trying to structure the win-win situation where possible, and knowing when to back off and compromise. Obviously, when done correctly, each person walks away feeling they were able to assertively get what they wanted and got the better end of the deal. Assertiveness is being able to take a stand and state one's opinion, but the devil is in the details.

Weaknesses Associated with Low Levels of Assertiveness:

Low levels of assertiveness indicate difficulty in expressing feelings, beliefs, taking a stand, and defending one's rights. These people are often shy, avoid contact with others, are submissive, and overcontrolled. The "so what" of this is that weakness in this area can equate to one being less than successful in life's transactions than what we are truly capable of. Additionally, our own behaviors and mannerisms send unconscious messages to others who are trying to get a "read" on us. The message often reads "take advantage of me." Humans, like animals that live in social groups, transmit instructions to others that relate what you think of yourself and how others should treat you. In social situations, other people can instinctively pick up on this very quickly. For example, one of the authors was seeing a third grader who was overweight, had been made fun of by others, got into a fight, and was suspended from school. His perplexing question was that this was exactly what happened at his previous school. He thought that with his move to a new school, things would be different; but alas, first day on the playground, others got their read on him and fell in line — it was if it was written on his forehead. He came to the realization that people treated him this way because he let them, and since their desired intent was to get him upset, so that he would chase them (hence get in trouble), why should they quit — it worked every time. Obviously, this example points to the interaction of self-regard (the ability to respect and accept oneself as basically good) with independence (the ability to be self-directed and self-controlled in one's thinking and action, and to be free of emotional dependency) and assertiveness. Examine the levels of the first two factors in relation to the assertiveness. Some may find it difficult in being assertive because of poor self-regard coupled with a degree of emotional dependency. For example, I'm afraid to assert myself and tell others what I really think because I'm not very popular to begin with; they might get mad at me, but I need their approval and friendship.

From time to time, we all can feel those butterflies in our stomach at some point in our life, whether it be anxiety from having to speak in public to being in a social situation with total strangers. The bottom line is that learning to deal with and tame these "butterflies" can greatly improve our lot in life. Physically, anxiety is a normal response of the body associated with the stress response to a perceived danger or threat, with the associated demands for coping from the body. The brain signals the hypothalamus, which stimulates the production of adrenal hormones cortisol and adrenaline, and then the famous "fight or flight" physiological response goes into action. Once these "stress hormones" enter the bloodstream, the heart rate accelerates, muscles contract, and we begin to sweat. Our faces flush, we develop sweaty hands, and we begin to feel the infamous "butterflies in the stomach." This is enough to propel many to the classic avoidance technique, avoiding those "sticky" situations that evoke this response within us. The problem is that avoidance costs us plenty, causing us to miss out on opportunity: in relationships, career advancement, and in other areas of life, depriving us of pleasurable feelings typically associated with accomplishment and success. Underlying this seems to be fear. Fear perhaps of being embarrassed or that we will evoke the negative judgments of others. We fear that we will get *them* angry, evoke their wrath, contempt, or even worse, ridicule. Perhaps we fear that we'll say something that will make us look stupid or foolish. So, we continue to avoid when we should be doing the opposite. We should be confronting and dealing with these anxiety-producing fears, which are usually based upon faulty beliefs to begin with.

There are a number of simple techniques that can be used to deal with those fear-provoking situations that we try to avoid because of lack of assertiveness. One such technique was developed by Albert Ellis, who was previously mentioned. This cognitive-behavioral strategy is called "ABCDE":

A What is the activating event that we seek to avoid...the fear-producing event? Such an event might be, for example, giving public speeches.

B What is the irrational belief about this situation? "I know I'll mess up, they'll laugh at me, and that would be horrible!"

C What are the consequences of this irrational belief that keeps me from speaking in public and causes me to be relegated to a role of silence in staff meetings?

D Dispute the irrational belief. Decatastrophyize it. "Where is it written, and who says that I will mess up?" "Will people really laugh at me, and would that be so horrible?"

E Examine the evidence to the contrary. "I have spoken to small groups of people and haven't messed up." "Even when I did stumble a bit with my lines, no one laughed at me...after all, we're all human." "And even if I did mess up, it would not be so horrible...it wouldn't be a catastrophe."

There are numerous other ideas and techniques that can be used to enhance assertiveness, many of which are quite simple, though effective. Rehearse and develop the skills that you feel you struggle with. With respect to overcoming fear related to giving public speeches for example, simply practice giving a speech by yourself and perhaps videotaping it. Then deliver it to a small circle of friends with whom you are comfortable. Then gradually progress to larger groups. To develop these skills further, it is possible to join a group like Toastmasters International, do some reading on how to give an effective presentation, or take a course.

The bottom line is that we have to face and conquer those things that we have difficulty with, which not only make us fearful, but rob us of living at a level consistent with our true capability.

Potential Opportunities Associated with Average Levels of Assertiveness:

The opportunities to improve skills in the assertiveness domain are many. In addition to those already mentioned, we will discuss a number of other simple and effective techniques below, as well as refer the reader to even more possibilities at the end of this section and in the Appendix. The message that we want to convey here is that it is possible to improve assertiveness, and the reward in doing so is that it opens the possibility of taking a more active role in your future.

Working on a *mission statement*, either personal or organizational, provides us with a template of purpose and allows us to more assertively take a role in shaping our destiny versus being a hapless victim. Laura Jones, author of *The Path: Creating Your Personal Mission Statement for Work and Life* and *Jesus, CEO: Using Ancient Wisdom for Visionary Leadership*, lists some excellent basic points on how to develop a personal mission statement:

- Keep it short and to the point. It should be understood by a 12-year-old. If it's too long and overly detailed, it can't provide straightforward direction.
- Recite it by memory. We must keep it at the center of our focus to give reason to our actions.
- Eliminate excuses, such as "my job is my mission." A job is part of a mission, but a mission is larger than a job. "My role is my mission" — women tend to define themselves more in terms of relationships and roles, whereas men more in what they do professionally. The danger coming from overinvesting in roles is that they change — career changes, divorce, kids grow up, death, and so on. What do you do then if those were your only missions in life? "I am not important enough to have a mission in life." — don't assume your mission has to be grand — a mission statement helps you make the greatest possible impact, versus being a victim or passive participant in what life hands out.
- Clear out past personality influences. Whose mission are you living? Yours, your parents, or your boss's? The idea is that having a mission is about doing what excites you...what you are passionate about.

These suggestions prompt the obvious: How do I go about this? Jones suggests some basic questions to ask:

- What is it that inspires me? Passion is power. The mission statement should include gifts, talents, and abilities, woven to encompass a lifetime of activities. This allows all our activities to flow and relate to the mission.
- What is my vision about myself? What is your unique selling point? What we think about ourselves is reflected in everything we say or

do. What are you reflecting about yourself?

- What are my resources? Take an inventory...talents, gifts, hobbies, training, financial resources, skills, and most specifically the people who have these as well. The art of networking with these people to tap or engage them in helping facilitate your mission is important.
- Constantly reevaluate and revise your mission statement. Live it every day...missions evolve over time...finding and living your mission is the key to living a more fulfilled life, and assertively beginning to stand up for what's important to you in that regard.

The idea from all this is that before we can really begin to be assertive in life, we have to build a foundation of what's important to us and worth defending or seeing happen. Anyone can learn to champion a losing cause, but the skill is assertively being an active participant in shaping the fulfillment of mission, using skill in assertiveness at the opportune times. The visual image for this should be the use of "retro-rockets" in space modules. The retro-rockets tend to be "fired" or "asserted," producing thrust in an opposite direction to the motion of the craft, slowing down a descent to decelerate the craft for reentry. The point is that they are powerful and are not used wastefully, but used only at the opportune time, necessary to correct and control the progress along a planned course. Without them, the "nonassertive" craft would not have this control, being pulled down the path that gravity determined, which would be to the ultimate detriment of the craft.

It's not always easy to deal with difficult people. Dealing with such people, like overcoming the fear of public speaking, requires well-developed assertiveness, and this type of experience provides us with an excellent laboratory to both examine our level of assertiveness and to improve it. It is important to deal with these people based upon reason and not emotions. To keep this rational perspective, it is important to not get "hooked." More specifically: "Don't take it personally." Moreover, the line gets drawn in the sand, and the situation escalates when we tend to see ourselves as a target. Difficult people often act this way in many settings. If it is true that most behavior is goal-directed, we have to contemplate what the person's goal might be at any point in time. Gini Scott, author of *Resolving Conflict: With Others and Within Yourself*, notes that different types of people call for different responses. She notes several interesting types of people and some basic ideas for dealing with them in an assertive manner:

- **The Kamikaze** — This is the type who bullies, blows up, and goes for head-on confrontations. Trying to reason with this type of person in the middle of an outburst isn't effective. The strategy here is to allow them to vent, control your tone of voice, stating your position firmly and maintaining self-control and composure. The saying that "a soft answer turneth away wrath" is wise. Second, giving in on small matters can at times allow them to save face and may possibly defuse the situation.

- **The Sneak** — This type person isn't overly aggressive but undermines by criticism disguised as humor. The most effective strategy here is to expose the undercover tactics, but without getting emotional. The idea is to confront the behavior preferably with others around: "Was that meant as a put down?" If they deny it, cite your evidence calmly. Eventually, these people tend to seek other targets.

- **The Whiner** — These people complain in order to seek attention, because they feel powerless. No one listens to them or takes them seriously. With this type, the best approach is to use active listening, reflecting what you heard them say, then shifting to a problem solving mode: "What is your plan?" or "So, what do you plan to do?"

- **The Sulker** — This type typically sits and sulks in silence. They are best dealt with by not begging them to tell you what's wrong. They should be confronted with open-ended questions offering them the chance to elaborate: "What's your feeling about this?" You can also share your gut intuition in a low-key nonthreatening way: "You seem to be withdrawn, and I was wondering if it had anything to do with my canceling your vacation request?"

- **The Procrastinator** — With those people who typically procrastinate, the best tactic is to ask about the reason for the delay, and perhaps brainstorm ways to resolve the problem and get things going.

- **The Naysayer** — This type is reminiscent of the young child who is in the throws of the "terrible twos." They are typically negative by nature and automatically reject what others have to say and request of them. The most positive thing about their style is that it often points out the potential faults in what is being discussed and may provide the opportunity to troubleshoot. In most other encounters with this type, it's best to confront their behavior by asking what is meant by it and, perhaps, suggesting that it might indicate that they're not open to change or fear failure. Reassure them that you are prepared to deal with problems when they arise.

Roger Fisher, author of *Beyond Maschiavelli: Tools for Coping With Conflict*, offers some basic points worthy of note when involved in a disagreement:

- Take control of your emotions. The idea here is to be aware of and take control of your emotions in order to remain rational in your response versus being emotionally hijacked and allowing your emotions to take control of you.
- Try to understand the other person and situation. Use empathy to try to understand the other person's position — reverse roles for a moment. This aids in negotiation and possibly leads to compromises that we would not be willing to make otherwise.
- Communicate more effectively. Avoid long speeches. Practice short, clear statements, pausing for response, and listening. A good tactic here is to take responsibility for misunderstandings, versus blaming. This is a sign of strength, self-confidence, and self-control.
- Persuade, versus using coercion. Make your case on logic, versus an attack. A saying that illustrates this point is, "Be soft on people...hard on the problem."

One of the reasons that we often fail to get what we want is that we view these interchanges as all-or-nothing situations. The shift should be to look for middle ground. Mark Hansen and Jack Canfield, authors of the best seller *Chicken Soup for the Soul* and *A Second Helping of Chicken Soup for the Soul*, offer a few pointers in progressing towards getting what you want. The first is to address the underlying fear. Many people fail to be assertive in asking for what they want because of fear of rejection, humiliation, and so forth. The idea is to focus on the merits of your request, not how you will appear to others. This tactic can help banish these initial fears. Closely associated with this response is that before we try to sell others, we have to sell ourselves. This involves another emotional and personal skill called self-regard and also a degree of gumption…determination. The idea is that attitude, not aptitude, will determine altitude — or, another way of putting it is that we are what we think. Attitudes are more important than facts. History is replete with examples of people succeeding despite the facts — the naysayers that said that they couldn't. If we don't convince ourselves, how convincing can we be to others. Here self-regard is tempered with the skill of reality testing, reminding us that we do not get everything we want when we want it. Instead, we should note this from the beginning, organize our thoughts, and ask from the heart. A request made with enthusiasm and conviction is hard to resist. Asking in an enthusiastic manner and voice, and maintaining steady eye contact shows you mean business, but at the same time communicates respect. Finally, to be realistic, we have to be prepared to possibly deal with resistance. The idea is that resistance is not a dead end, merely a continuing conversation, and that no matter what the outcome is, gratitude (the art of saying thank you) will leave the other person more open to giving you what you ask at some time in the future.

Threats Associated with Very Low Levels of Assertiveness:

Weakness in the area of assertiveness limits one's ability to express feelings, beliefs, thoughts, disagree, and take a stand, especially when it is emotionally difficult or when one has something to lose by doing so. Limitations in assertiveness have a bleedover effect on other emotional and social factors like self-regard, independence, interpersonal relationship, and ultimately self-actu-alization. The ultimate threat this can pose is the risk of being acted upon instead of having some ability to shape the outcome of events and situations. The idea here is that nothing can have power over us unless we choose to let it. Passivity as compared to assertiveness tends to relegate one to lose-win scenarios. Since this weakness tends to denote one as an "easy mark," it can signal the "sharks" to initiate the feeding frenzy. From a corporate perspective, it connotes a lack of strategic direction and purpose, akin to a rudderless ship drifting with the winds and the tides of chance versus actively managing their destiny. Today's successful companies focus on "co-opetition" (cooperative competition) and the win-win scenario, versus competition and the win-lose scenario. The focus tends to be akin to symbiosis, which is a process by which two or more organisms increase their chances of ultimate survival by cooperating. Witness Microsoft-Apple, American-Russian Space Station ventures, Ford-Mazda, GM-Toyota, and so forth. The future will require corporate assertiveness — being capable of doing something about a situation versus being a victim of happenstance. These co-opetitive arrangements allow both parties this chance. Finally, this negates triangulation. In family systems theory, the idea is that when there is conflict or anxiety between two parties, the tendency is to triangulate with a third party instead of dealing directly with the person we have the difficulty with. The goal of therapy in many cases becomes helping people detriangulate and deal directly versus talking through and ventilating to a third party. When this is translated to the corporate world, it means dealing with the competition directly and structuring a co-opetitive arrangement where possible, versus triangulating and venting to a third party (like the federal government) on how they should be playing fair.

Bottom Line Suggestions for Improving Assertiveness

"Personal Remedies":

- Record specific situations and how you usually handle them.
- Think how it would feel if it were easier for you to more openly assert what you feel, think, and want.
- There's nothing wrong about expressing yourself, as long as you don't hurt anyone in the process.
- Take a specific situation, and ask someone you trust for advice on the assertive way to handle the situation.
- Learn to recognize when others are making unreasonable demands of you, and don't be afraid to say "no" when you have to.
- Try doing something that you didn't do in the past because you were too embarrassed to do it.
- The next time that you are in a group, say what you want to say and say it slowly and clearly — nothing will happen to you, and others will probably respect you more for doing it.
- Pick out which emotions are more difficult for you to express and then rehearse expressing them with someone you feel safe with.

- When something makes you feel happy, tell someone how you feel and why.
- The next time you feel sad, tell someone close to you how you are feeling and why.

"Group Remedies":

- Encourage people to express themselves more at work, to say what they think and to tell others how they feel about things.
- In meetings, encourage the more bashful and timid to contribute — tell them that you are interested in hearing what everyone has to say.
- Actively solicit and encourage the opinions of others.
- Facilitate group interaction and the sharing of ideas.
- If someone looks like they're having a bad day, ask what's happening and if they would like to talk about it.
- Organize a group at work, or perhaps a retreat, in which you can discuss assertiveness and how to improve it.
- Explain what is meant by "assertiveness" and why it's important for one's overall ability to effectively cope with daily demand.
- Emphasize why improving this skill will have a positive effect on the overall effectiveness and productivity of the organization as a whole.
- Discuss the importance of expressing what they feel and standing up for their rights in a constructive manner.
- Tell the group that there is nothing wrong or bad about telling others what they think and how they feel. They need not be embarrassed about saying what they want to say, convey, and do as long as it does not harm others.
- Then direct the role-playing to expressing their opinion about something in the work setting (like a simulated staff meeting).

Independence

Independence is the ability to be self-directed and self-controlled in one's thinking and actions and to be free of emotional dependency. Independent people are self-reliant in planning and making decisions. They may, however, seek and consider other people's opinions before making the right decision for themselves in the end — consulting others is not necessarily a sign of dependency. Independence is, essentially, the ability to function autonomously versus needing protection and support — independent people avoid clinging to others in order to satisfy their needs. The ability to be independent rests on one's degree of self-confidence, inner strength, and desire to meet expectations and obligations. The ability to be decisive is dependent upon a strong sense of independence, and decisiveness is considered to be a very important managerial competency based on research conducted by the US Office of Personnel Management (Corts & Gowing, 1992).

Strengths Associated with High Levels of Independence:

People who have high levels of independence tend to be self-reliant and autonomous in their thinking and actions; these people may ask for and consider the advice of others, but they rarely depend upon others to make important decisions or do things for them. These people rarely cling to other people. Individuals or groups who are considered to be highly independent, demonstrate a sense of confidence and inner strength that is characterized by positive self-regard and durable self-esteem. These individuals or groups possess a requisite characteristic for living on the cutting edge. They are generally free from the need for approval and emotional dependence upon others. These are the people who can live life on the outposts of the frontier of the future. Individuals or groups who are evaluated as being highly independent are the free thinkers that can be an asset to any organization. Instead of seeing a simple, one or two ways of doing things, they can see multiple possibilities and are not afraid of taking the risks and failures associated with trying to find a better way. Based on our research, senior managers demonstrate a significantly high level of independence in comparison to the general population.

The balance that is necessary to keep this strength in perspective is a sense of humility to avoid arrogance or narcissism. An average to high level of social responsibility tends to balance this area, as do high levels of empathy and interpersonal relationship. Also, this factor also needs to be balanced by efficient reality testing.

Weaknesses Associated with Low Levels of Independence:

A weakness in this area denotes a certain sense of dependence upon others, perhaps a tenuous self-esteem and lack of confidence. A weakness in this area is like a deer caught in the headlights. It can freeze us, whether individually or as a group, in our tracks and make us afraid to take the risks associated with movement. Weakness here, especially if profound, can also alienate others. A profound need for the approval of others, constant need for validation, and rechecking can be an irritant to others, especially for those who possess high levels of independence and don't have this need for validation. Weaknesses here are frequently due to self-concepts. If we tell ourselves that we will fail, we can't do it on our own, we have to have other's approval, we set ourselves up for a roller coaster ride based upon the fickle opinions of others. Once again, this emphasizes the importance of being free of emotional dependency, of being self-directed (versus other-directed) and self-controlled in our thinking and actions.

Weaknesses in this area are frequently accompanied by weaknesses in self-regard, emotional self-awareness, assertiveness, and self-actualization. It must be noted that a healthy sense of *interdependence* is necessary in today's communities of practice common in the business world. However, it is important to point out that this is cooperation with and interdependence upon others versus dependence upon them.

Potential Opportunities Associated with Average Levels of Independence:

The opportunities to improve weaknesses begin with thinking logically about the implications of dependence and interdependence. To do well in this world, especially in today's corporate ecosystem, it requires a certain degree of *interdependence* or *mutual dependence* on others. However, as was pointed out, this is quite different from *dependence*, which is typically a one way relationship (i.e., one person being dependent upon another). In thinking logically about a tendency towards dependence, let's start with dependent *behavior* itself: "What need in my life does this type of behavior meet?" If we begin with an assumption that most behavior is goal-directed, what would the goal be in being dependent upon others? There are a number of possibilities: (1)

dependence for approval based on lack of positive self-regard ("I don't think highly of myself, and my only worth is based on how others' evaluate me and what they think of me"), (2) dependence for support based on lack of assertiveness ("I want you to come with me to talk to the boss"), (3) dependence for direction based on lack of self-actualization ("What do you think I should do with my life?"), (4) dependence for control based on lack of impulse control ("I can't control my spending, so you take control of the checkbook"), (5) dependence for emotional insight based on lack of emotional self-awareness ("I can't tell when I'm getting angry, and you know how I get, so just don't get me upset"). These types of behaviors all are directed at meeting a basic need or reaching a certain goal, but this also combines with a certain lack of responsibility. For example, "I can't take care of the checkbook, so you do it for me" or "You have to take care of me because I can't do it myself." We need to look at some of these behaviors and thought processes at a deeper level in order to understand exactly what's going on and to put things in their proper perspective. To do this, we have to ask a number of questions. Where did this need for reassurance and approval come from? What meaning did I assign to this event? Is that true or not? What belief did I form around this interpretation of that event? What emotion followed? What behavior followed? A practical example to illustrate this point is that of a young engineer who had a constant need for approval from her boss, failing to initiate even minute changes or actions without checking with the boss. This led to a certain degree of frustration on the boss's part, to the point that she began isolating herself from the young engineer, which further rattled the self-esteem of this young lady. She eventually sought help. In therapy, she traced this behavior back to her mother being very critical of her in almost every aspect of her life. She deeply wanted to please her mother and basically resigned control over many aspects of her life, rather than make the wrong decision and have her mother displeased with her choice. The meaning the young lady assigned to these events was that "I must please people in authority" and "I can't make good decisions on my own." The feelings that followed this faulty logic were ones of worthlessness, sadness, and despair. The behavior that these feelings drove was a constant need for reassurance and approval from authority figures. In therapy, the young engineer began to challenge these faulty meanings with questions like "Who says that I can't make good decisions?" and "Who says that I can possibly please everyone all the time?" The result was that she slowly began to realize that her dependence upon others was based on an illogical need from the very beginning. In conclusion, we return to the following model: What is the dependent behavior? What need in my life does that meet (the goal of the behavior)? Are there any events that I can trace this behavior back to? What meaning did I assign to these events? What feelings or emotions followed my assigning those meanings to those events? What behaviors follow my experiencing these feelings? This involves some introspection, and, perhaps, some help in learning to examine our dysfunctional dependencies in an open and honest manner, but this search is well worth the freedom that we can experience from these dependencies.

Threats Associated with Very Low Levels of Independence:

The threat from being overly dependent is obvious, especially, for the dependent individual. It basically typecasts one in a role of dependency upon others and being subject to riding an emotional roller coaster in response to the whims of others. This also has a damaging effect on relationships, usually alienating others from dependent people, especially people that are independent and have high self-regard and a strong sense of self. Many dysfunctional relationships are based upon a symbiosis in this area — one person enabling the other to be and remain dependent so that person can take on the role of the independent partner who takes responsibility for the life of the dependent partner. This type of relationship is frequently found when one partner is a substance abuser. These relationships can become co-dependent. One needs the other to be responsible for them, and the other needs to be needed in this way. These are very unhealthy relationships for many reasons, one of which is that dependency does not lead to self-actualization. Behavior theory proposes that behavior that is not reinforced will not be repeated. If we return to the idea that behavior is goal-directed, we then have to ask what's reinforcing dependent behavior? Instead of actually helping these people by spoon-feeding them, we are actually harming them because we are reinforcing their dependency, which means it's likely to be repeated. If we look at models from the animal world, the approach to curb this behavior is twofold. Eagles will feed their young until the point when they instinctively know that their young have the skills and abilities to feed themselves, and then they quit. This is essentially based on an idea of training and skill verification. This is what parents and supervisors are required to do. Once we can absolutely know that the individual has the requisite skill, then it becomes more of a "tough love" approach — not reinforcing this behavior by allowing them to do it on their own and not rescuing them from the consequences of their actions. By not reinforcing earlier dependent behavior, they are placing them in a situation of either doing it for themselves or finding someone else they can manipulate to do it for them. Finally, dependent behavior can be a two-way street. It takes a minimum of two people to play out this type of behavior within relationships: one to initiate the dependent behavior and the other to allow it to happen.

Bottom Line Suggestions for Improving Independence

"Personal Remedies":

- Make a list of situations in which you feel more independent and situations in which you are more dependent, and try to understand what that tells you about yourself.
- Ask yourself how it makes you feel to be more dependent on the one hand and more independent on the other?
- Although there may be advantages to being dependent at times, being independent makes you feel stronger and gives you more control of your life.
- In general, try to be more self-directed in your thinking and decision making.
- Make an attempt to be more on your own and to do things without outside help.
- There is nothing wrong with asking others for their advice and opinions on different things, but do not over-rely on others to the

point where you don't make your own choices and decisions.

- Remember that others can make suggestions, but you make the actual decisions in your life because you know what's best for you more than anyone else.
- When working on something, encourage yourself to do as much of the task as you can on your own by breaking the task down into smaller steps that are easier for you to do. Before asking for help, ask yourself if you can do the task on your own. If the answer is yes, then proceed on your own. You may find that you only need help with one small aspect of the task rather than with the entire task.
- In general, rely more on yourself than on others.
- Avoid clinging to people for emotional support. Try to derive more support from within, from your own inner strength. Believe in yourself more.

"Group Remedies":

- Encourage others to take on more responsibility and to exercise their own judgment, while still adhering to protocol and emphasizing teamwork — create a balance between individual thinking and action on the one hand and teamwork on the other.
- Allow subordinates to play a larger role in planning, decision making, supervision, and management as much as possible. Specifically, encourage the more dependent workers to contribute more in these and in other activities.
- Encourage an exchange of ideas. Emphasize that everyone has something to offer and that everyone can learn from everyone else. Stress the importance of the collective use of individual ideas.
- Ask the more dependent people at work what they think about the task at hand, how they would deal with it, which decisions would they make, and so forth. Praise their initiative.
- Organize a group at work, or perhaps a retreat, in which you can discuss independence and ways to improve the areas that need to be improved.
- Explain what is meant by independence and why it's important for one's ability to effectively and successfully cope with daily demands.

Emphasize why improving this skill will increase the overall productivity of the organization as a whole.

- Tell them that there's nothing wrong with asking advice from time to time, but it is important to make the big decisions and to do things more on their own because they know what's best for them.
- Convey to them that one generally feels stronger and has a better sense of accomplishment when doing things independently.
- Discuss a few easy ways to do things on their own — like dividing tasks into smaller more manageable chunks, seeing if they can take on some of the easier tasks on their own, only asking for advice when they get stuck.
- Encourage them to talk openly about where they think they are more independent, and where less and why. Try to encourage them to talk about how independent they feel they are at work and what they can do to be more independent.
- Have them role-play typical situations at work in which they can experiment with being more independent — work on different scenarios of independent behavior and give them positive feedback for suggesting more independent ways of doing things.

Self-Actualization

Self-actualization pertains to the ability to realize one's potential capacities. This component of emotional, personal, and social intelligence is manifested by becoming involved in pursuits that lead to a more meaningful, rich, and full life. Striving to actualize one's potential involves developing interests and enjoyable activities that can lead to a lifelong effort and enthusiastic commitment to long-term goals; excitement and passion about one's interests energizes and motivates one to continue these interests. Self-actualization is an ongoing, dynamic process of striving toward maximum development of one's abilities, capabilities, and talents. This factor is associated with persistently trying to do one's best and trying to improve oneself in general; this leads to feelings of self-satisfaction. Self-actualization is similar to the famous recruiting line of the US Army: "Be all you can be." It is also knowing one's preferences, knowing where one wants to go and why, being self-directed, being committed to long-term goals and lifelong dreams, having vision, and being achievement-oriented. It is important to note that self-direction and vision are considered to be valuable managerial competencies by the US Office of Personnel Management (Corts & Gowing, 1992).

Abraham Maslow was the first psychologist to research self-actualization; his famous study of this construct began in 1935 and continued for approximately half a century. Within the context of Maslow's classic hierarchy of needs, self-actualization represents the pinnacle of the pyramid. According to this hierarchy, basic needs have to be met first before one can address the higher-order needs like self-actualization. Physiological needs are the most basic and the first to be met followed by needs for safety; safety needs are then followed by satisfying one's needs for belongingness and trust. Self-actualization is the last need to be satisfied as was previously mentioned. The idea is that in order to realize one's potential, one must first satisfy all of these other lower-order needs. Although many people struggle to realize their potential capability, the vast majority of us do not succeed in self-actualizing to any great degree. This is evidenced by millions of individuals living lives beneath their true capabilities in a self-imposed quagmire. This ultimately leads to a general sense of unfulfillment and a lowering of expectations in order to adjust to the sad reality of not succeeding in doing what one wanted to do in life. These people remain where they are for the rest of their life with fleeting thoughts of what they could have been.

Strengths Associated with High Levels of Self-Actualization:

Self-actualizing people are able to realize their potential capabilities and become involved in pursuits that lead to interesting, exciting, and meaningful lives. These people have a good idea of where they are going, or want to go, and why. We have found that this factor is significantly developed in most successful senior managers. Whether for an individual or an organization, self-actualization represents a sense of direction and purpose — a road map of sorts. Strength in this area equates to a sense of fulfillment that goes beyond materialistic measures of success. Victor Frankl, the author of *Man's Search for Meaning*, made many of his observation's about the meaning of life in a Nazi concentration camp. After losing everything in the worst possible conditions experienced by human beings, he came to the realization that *a sense of meaning* is the most important driving force in life. Frankl saw this as a belief in a purpose greater than the drive for day-to-day survival. As defined above, self-actualization leads to and is energized by a sense of meaning.

In the history of mankind, those who made a lasting impact on the world had an undying sense of vision. Perhaps one of the most quoted individuals of our times who spoke of his dream was Martin Luther King. His famous speech "I have a dream" and reference to having been to the "mountaintop" indicated a clarity of purpose and a single-minded determination that inspired followers to go on, even in the face of adversity.

It is important to note that many cultures have placed a great deal of importance on self-actualization, which is often referred to by such terms as *becoming* or *enlightenment*.

Weaknesses Associated with Low Levels of Self-Actualization:

Weakness in self-actualization indicates a sense of emptiness that characterizes many. Weaknesses in this area imply a lack of direction, lack of purpose, lack of a dream, lack of vision, and a myopic view towards life in general. This is like being lost in the middle of a dense, dark forest without a compass. It's virtually impossible to find one's way without several missteps along the way. In essence, individuals or businesses that possess low levels of self-actualization can't see the forest for the trees. As was previously alluded to, this is probably one of the ultimate tragedies of mankind. A saying from the Bible summarizes the true consequence of this: "My people perish for lack of vision." People who are deficient in this area possess certain basic, though undeveloped, abilities, but fail to realize their true capabilities.

Irrespective of the reason or reasons for weaknesses in this area, it ultimately involves a sense of choice. The choice towards self-actualization is the choice to do something to make something happen, versus seeing oneself as a hapless victim of chance that the winds of destiny blow whither they will. A cartoon that illustrates this involved two starved, emaciated vultures sitting on a limb in a barren desert. The punch line showed one vulture turning to the other commenting "Wait heck! I'm fixing to make something happen!" Vultures typically have to wait for things to happen, as do many people in life, versus those who take an active role in shaping their destiny.

Not doing the things that one can do and wants to do leads to frustration. People may not know what they want to achieve because they are confused about themselves in general and what they want to do in life. Others may know what they want to accomplish in life but are unable to realize their potential for various reasons. For example, typical symptoms of depression include a withdrawal from interests, curtailment of personal pursuits, low motivation or lack of drive, not trying to improve oneself, feeling useless, feeling dissatisfied with what one is presently doing and with one's life in general.

Potential Opportunities Associated with Average Levels of Self-Actualization:

The opportunity to improve weaknesses in this area begins with our ability to change our attitudes. A few well-known sayings illustrate the importance of attitudes with this regard: "*attitudes are more important than facts,*" "*if you aim at nothing, you'll hit it every time,*" "*your attitude, not your aptitude, will determine your altitude,*" and so forth.

Jim Collins, co-author of *Built to Last: Successful Habits of Visionary Companies*, suggests that the idea of being a *lifelong learning person* is what's needed for this type of change to take place. Collins notes that to have to ask *why you need to put learning objectives before performance objectives* is like asking for a financial justification for breathing (*Inc. Magazine*, August 1997). This need of lifelong learning creates *a lifelong student*, who should be forever asking questions and continuously expressing a desire to learn. Collins cites John Gardner, author of *Self-Renewal: The Individual and the Innovative Society*, as saying "Don't set out in life to be an interesting person...set out to be an interested person." The difference in motives is illustrated by thinking for a moment how one's life and the lives of organizations would be different if their time, energy, and resources were organized around learning versus performance. This involves a continuous quest for knowledge and requires never becoming satisfied that one has reached the top and can now retire as the *expert* (which is a sure prescription for atrophy if not rigor mortis!). More than two millennia before Collins and Gardner, Socrates wrote that "the unquestioned life is not worth the living."

Improving in this area is similar to the process of "mastery" spoken about in the once popular TV martial arts series *Kung Fu*. In the series, the student would always ask the master "when"...inquiring as to when he would be considered trained. In each instance the master's response included a specific mastery marker such as "when you can grab these pebbles out of my hand" or "when you can walk across the rice paper without tearing it." The first point is that one of life's richest rewards is the *journey* on the road towards personal mastery, although we may never fully get there. The second point in this analogy is that mastery isn't something you get simply by attending a weekend seminar — it's a *process* that takes time. The third point is *practice*. The master answered the student's question of "when" by illustrating the gap between the skills that the student presently possessed and what was required. The fourth point is *the master* himself. Without the right master, teacher, coach, or mentor to guide you, you could be wasting your time. With regard to this, you must ask: *Who has achieved what you want to achieve*? and *Who is willing to share this one on one*? This personal relationship is very important, and the master should spend time not only telling you what you do wrong, but also what you do right. Not only is it important that the student trusts the master, but having faith in this special partnership, with someone who is greater than we are, is critical and even assumes a near spiritual quality at times.

Always be ready to *learn from others*. In a sense, most of what we are is borrowed from others...our parents, teachers, mentors, and so forth. It is said that Sam Walton, one of the founders of Wal-Mart was a master at this, constantly inquisitive and learning about his craft (retailing) from others. An example of this appeared in *Inc. Magazine* in August 1997. A group of Brazilian businessmen, who had purchased a discount retailing chain, had written to ten US retailing CEOs asking for an appointment. Walton was the only one to grant an appointment. The Brazilians were interested in learning from Walton since they didn't know much about the retailing business. In addition to the questions that the Brazilians asked, Walton pummeled them with questions as well. As a result of this encounter, a joint venture with Wal-Mart was later launched in South America.

Be willing to tolerate lots of failure along the way. Failure is only crippling when we fail to learn from it. Doug Englebart, founder of the Bootstrap Institute and considered to be an icon of the digital revolution, addresses this point: "The rate at which a person can mature is directly proportional to the embarrassment he can tolerate...and I've tolerated lots" (*US News and World Report*, May 20 1996).

Don't always accept others' opinions of what you can and can't accomplish. Joseph Ellis, author of *American Sphinx: The Character of Thomas Jefferson*, noted that Thomas Jefferson was such a person. Many influential leaders of the day thought that the colonies couldn't survive the Revolutionary War. Jefferson believed that the break with England was inevitable, that the institutions established in the US after the war would survive, and that the US was destined to become one of the world's greatest nation. His prophetic words cited in the Declaration of Independence still are a cornerstone to this belief: "We hold these truths to be self-evident..."

In addition to what was previously said about self-actualization, you have to have a sense of *devotion* or *love* for what you do if you want to succeed. In life, it's never a matter of not enough time, it's a matter of priority. We always seem to have plenty of time for *what's important* to us, but mysteriously not enough for something we don't value as much. It helps tremendously if we are *passionate* about what we do. Dr. Bernie Siegel, a former professor of surgery at Yale University School of Medicine and author of *Love, Medicine and Miracles*, noted some characteristics of "exceptional" cancer patients. These exceptional patients tended to do better emotionally and physically than others. The two salient traits he felt that separated them from the others were *inspiration* and *information*. Specifically, with regard to inspiration he noted the need for *a sense of meaning* from work, daily activities and relationships, noting that people who dislike what they do often get ill or fare worse as cancer patients than those who enjoy what they do.

Michael Levine, author of *Take it from Me: Practical and Inspiring Career Advice from the Celebrated and the Successful*, discussed several common strategies of the more than 300 people he interviewed for this book. These people were some America's most prominent and successful people. First, these people know where they are going. Second, they throw themselves into whatever they do. The idea here is that they don't just show up to work — they throw themselves into it and aren't satisfied with just being good enough, average, or ordinary. Third, they take the initiative. There is often a fine balance between seizing the initiative and avoiding being impulsive. Many people avoid taking the initiative because they are afraid to take a risk when they might fail or make a mistake. Success doesn't come from making the fewest mistakes — it comes from getting the results. Obviously, the moral of this story is that you don't get results without initiating some sort of action. Fourth, successful people are creative. They don't see things simplistically — they see alternatives. Key to this is that they ask questions: *What if...? Why? Can it be done another way?* A scenario to build skills in this way is to force yourself, and others, to come up with a number of ways to solve a particular problem or deal with a specific issue. Fifth, successful people are persistent but polite. Persistent to the point of being determined, but coupled with a sensitivity to others.

Rich Patino, coach and president of the Boston Celtics and co-author of *Success Is a Choice: Ten Steps to Overachieving in Business and Life*, lists some key points applicable to self-actualization. He believes that you must set big goals and see yourself achieving them. The opposite of this is reminiscent of the aforementioned saying that *if you aim at nothing, you will hit it every time.* To succeed, he also feels that you must be able to envision a better and more positive future. We have to see things in a positive light — being negative is an enemy of success. The following saying illustrates this point nicely: "As a man thinketh in his heart, so is he." We are what we think. If you envision yourself failing, why should you be surprised when it happens? It's important to bear in mind that we can't control the world, but we can control our attitude and responses. We need to program ourselves to be more positive. This is influenced by those with whom we associate. For example, being around people who are constantly pessimistic has a weighty effect on our outlook.

Finally, it's important to maintain a certain degree of creative tension and to avoid stress as much as possible. Creative tension is self-imposed and derived from our drive to achieve, while stress is the body's response to an external demand or perceived threat. Whereas a certain amount of creative tension is necessary to avoid "rustout" and to drive our efforts to self-actualize, too much stress causes "burnout."

Threats Associated with Very Low Levels of Self-Actualization:

The basic threat posed by low levels of self-actualization is like sailing in a ship without a rudder...one is moving but not in a purposeful direction and without the ability to steer a course. Individuals and corporations that suffer from this malady are perhaps going through the motions but are not experiencing a sense of fulfillment in what they do. This lack of fulfillment and enjoyment, in and of itself, is the fuel that drives those with higher levels of self-actualization; this fuel and internal engine is necessary to provide the drive and motivation necessary to develop a sense of being all that one can be. Without this sense of purpose, vision, or road map, many individuals and organizations frequently live and function at a level beneath their true capabilities. Possessing a low level of self-actualization can become an inertia or drag that traps these people and organizations preventing them from becoming what they are truly capable of being. This becomes a negative self-fulfilling prophecy and has the potential to turn into learned helplessness over a period of time. It can become a chronic no-win condition that is hard to pull out of. Providing a sense of purpose and vision to individuals or organizations low in this area is not easy, because, in many cases, it has become their model of the world. George Kelly, who developed the Personal Construct Theory, which is used in artificial intelligence and neural networks, came up with a theory about this. He suggested that *our behavior is influenced by the way we anticipate events* (Kelly, 1963). This means that our world is perceived in terms of the meaning we apply to it. The value of this theory lies in the implication that *we have the freedom to choose and apply a different meaning to the way we view ourselves, others, and the world we live in.* This means that we are able to apply alternative meanings to events in the past, present, and future, which means that we are not captives or prisoners of our past. This means that we can free ourselves from the anguish of past events and beliefs if we want by reconstruing and reinterpreting them. As individuals and organizations, we use our constructs to give meaning to the constant flow of events and beliefs. This construct system becomes a system of rules that allows us to act in the world with a reasonable expectation of being able to predict and, to some degree, have some control over events. When things match the expectations of our constructs, the system is validated and strengthened, and we experience positive emotions. On the other hand, when things don't turn out in a manner consistent with the working predictions of our construct system, we experience negative emotions and are forced to reconstrue the events or look for other ways to make sense of them. The implications of all this are: Who says that the meanings we assign to things are correct? This is where faulty logic comes in, acting like a computer virus, capable of corrupting our entire operating system and thus having a negative effect on output. The first step in changing this faulty logic system (e.g., "I'm no good at math; therefore, I must be stupid or dumb since others don't have this problem; therefore, I can't go to college; therefore, I won't try since it's no use anyway") is to challenge these assumptions. We must challenge them by forcing ourselves to reexamine the construct or belief (i.e. Who says it's so? Who says that's what it means? Where's the evidence to support that conclusion? Does the conclusion follow from the facts?). Much like computers, an individual's or organization's construct or operating system becomes their model of the world. It is through this that they filter input from their environment, and this forms the basis by which they determine the actions they must take in response to incoming information. The major threat with such a corrupted construct system is that we don't have the right road map for success — and the worst possible scenario is that we may have one for failure instead! This can become a death spiral both individually and organizationally that's hard to pull out of. This negative or faulty construct system discounts the visionary, optimistic, driven, and self-fulfilling outlook characteristic of the extraordinary, for a more myopic, inertia-bound view. The hope here is that those with this infectious sense of purpose, vision, and optimism can, through the power of being a positive Pygmalion, inspire others who struggle in this area to greater heights of achievement, pushing their envelope and expanding their world. In viewing the history of great turnarounds, whether it be in the corporate teams or athletic teams, it has always involved a leadership dynamic that refused to accept the prevailing constructs of the system they inherited, forcing them to think differently, expect to succeed, and consequently, do so.

Bottom Line Suggestions for Improving Self-Actualization

"Personal Remedies":

- Ask yourself how satisfied you are with the things that you are presently doing, with your interests.
- Make a list of all of the things that really interest you, then make a serious effort to get more involved in those things.
- Try to learn more about the things that you like doing. Collect more information about your interests. Talk to others who are working and involved in the things that you're interested in.
- Set aside a number of hours a week to pursue those things that are interesting and meaningful for you.
- When the opportunity provides itself, share your interests with others — tell people what interests you, tell them about what you are doing or want to do.
- If you're not happy with what you are presently doing, think of what you would like to and can possibly do. Seriously consider what you would really like to do in life.
- Set aside a list of things you want to do, then experiment with each one to see what suits you and your personality best.
- Take up an interest or hobby if you don't have one at the moment.
- Make a more concentrated effort to see where your skills and talents lie.
- Explore the possibility that there might be areas that you are not yet aware of, that could be of interest to you; you might discover that you have hidden interests and talents that you did not know of, which can give you a great deal of gratification and satisfaction.

"Group Remedies":

- Encourage the people you work with to learn more about their work — to gain a deeper knowledge about it.
- Ask others about their particular interests at work and what they would like to pursue more in depth if they could. Encourage them to talk more about what they are doing, what they like to do, and how

they would like develop their field even more so. Also encourage them to talk about what they like to do in their leisure time.

- Encourage them to acquire more knowledge (via reading, courses, electronic media), particularly when they show a keen interest in something.
- Provide opportunities for others to develop new skills and to pursue subsidiary interests and goals.
- Try to match what people are actually doing as closely as possible with what they like doing and what they are good at doing.
- Organize a group at work, or perhaps a retreat, in which you can discuss self-actualization and how to enhance this area.
- Explain what is meant by "self-actualization" and why this is important for the individual as well as for the organization.
- Explain why working towards self-actualization will have an overall positive effect on the productivity of the organization as a whole.
- Tell the group that self-actualization leads to a feeling accomplishment and satisfaction.
- In smaller groups, have them talk about their past and present interests, what they like doing and why, how they got interested in what they are doing, future plans, and how they would like to develop these interests further.
- Encourage them to talk about their short-term and long-term goals and what they are doing to accomplish them.

PART 2:
Interpersonal Skills

Interpersonal skills include *empathy*, *social responsibility*, and *interpersonal relationship*. People with well-developed skills in this area are often described as responsible and dependable individuals — they understand, interact, and relate well with others. These people function well in positions that require teamwork and interacting with others. Our research has demonstrated that well-developed interpersonal skills are significantly important for people involved in sales, customer service, public relations, human resources, employment counseling, and management. Interpersonal skills are considered to be one of the most important managerial competencies by the US Office of Personnel Management (Corts & Gowing, 1992; Gregory & Park, 1992).

Empathy

Empathy is the ability to be aware of, understand, and to appreciate the feelings of others. It is "tuning in" (being sensitive) to what, how, and why people feel the way they do. Being empathetic means being able to "emotionally read" other people. Empathetic people care about others, and show interest in and concern for others. This component encompasses a capacity for interpersonal warmth, involvement, attachment, and sensitivity. Empathy plays an important part in social awareness — being aware of others' feelings, needs, and concerns. This is considered to be an important managerial competency.

Strengths Associated with High Levels of Empathy:

High levels of this factor are indicative of people who are aware of and can appreciate the feelings of others; they are sensitive to others' feelings and can understand why they feel the way they feel. Our research findings have demonstrated that strength in this area is an essential trait for salespeople, employment counselors, psychologists, psychiatrists, and social workers. High levels of this factor identify people who are able to emotionally read others on the fly and make adjustments as necessary. Salespeople with high levels of empathy can read a "cold sale" and don't waste time on non-productive scenarios. Another area this plays out in corporate life is in interpersonal interactions. Empathetic individuals understand when it's time to say more, when it's time to stop, when it's time to assert oneself, and when it's time to pull back. Essentially, empathy is a critical social skill, akin to the eyes' relationship to the body. The eyes provide visual input to allow the brain to coordinate certain activities for maximum effect. For instance, the eyes of a house painter give feedback as to the color saturation and coverage of their brush strokes, the color match of the paint to the desired color, and so forth. In a sense, the eyes act as a feedback mechanism. Empathy acts much the same way allowing us to "read" (observe) others as events transpire, receive interpersonal input, and adjust our actions accordingly for maximum effect. Individuals with low levels of empathy are, in a sense, emotionally blind. The reason empathy is essential in business relationships, especially in interpersonal interactions, is that they call for a unique personal approach. Individuals high in empathy have learned which strategies and tactics to use with various types of people, knowing that no two are alike. They are able to read certain cues from the boss that signal anger and the cues that signal "tell me more." They are adept at using an almost intuitive sense of *angles*. These angles are the various strategies and approaches that need to be utilized with the various life situations they encounter, especially those of an interpersonal nature. The key skills in this area are the ability to read the *nonverbals* like tone of voice, facial expressions, posture, body movement, and so forth. This is why this skill is important for people working in sales and marketing, customer service, human resources, and similar areas as was previously mentioned. Individuals high in this area are often good facilitators and negotiators because empathy is a critical factor in interpersonal communication. Such people are skilled at reading the emotional topography of an event on the fly and directing or facilitating a transaction. Making use of this skill in business interactions is important in appropriately structuring the win-win scenarios. Individuals and groups high in empathy are adept at reading what seems to be important to the other party and structuring deals so that the other party feels that they got something in return for what they gave. This is especially critical in global business relationships that characterize today's corporate world, where culture plays heavily in success of certain transactions. Finally, from an organizational perspective, this skill is essential for strategic planning and processing input (feedback) from the environment. Strength in this skill means the ability to receive input, process it, and adjust actions accordingly. On the other hand, weaknesses in this skill characterize those organizations who just don't get it — those who haplessly make one blunder after another, by misjudging consumer needs and interests, or losing out in a business transaction for failure to read and respond adequately to the other parties' signals of "I don't see what's in it for us."

Weaknesses Associated with Low Levels of Empathy:

Weakness in this area spells real difficulty in effective interpersonal and business relationships. As indicated earlier, it is like being emotionally blind or emotionally tone deaf. Individuals or organizations with significant deficits in this area seem to ride emotionally rough shod over other parties and wonder "What? Was it something I said?" The point that we must grasp is that in the era of intellectual capital and knowledge workers, a requisite existence will be teams, webs, networking, alliances, and communities of practice. These relationships require orchestration as many are uneasy alliances of former competitors such as Apple-Microsoft and the USSR-US. The required skill in such relationships requires "shuttle diplomacy" — the ability to work the interests of both parties and arrange the win-win or *quid pro quo*. On the interpersonal side, significant weaknesses in this area tend to equate to walking through life as if it were a minefield, seemingly unable to avoid stepping on the land mines or setting off emotional trip wires. These difficulties frequently play out in intimate relations as well. Based on many years of experience in marital and family counseling, one of the co-authors has noticed that one of the more frequent complaints registered is, "He or she doesn't understand my feelings." An interesting aside is that certain occupational groups that tend to groom a sense of analytical thinking make it difficult for some of its adherents to turn it off when they go home. For example, from years of working with pilots, a common complaint heard by one of the co-authors from the spouse in marital counseling deals with the seeming absence of empathy or emotions. The spouses typically note: "I just want to talk to him…I don't want him to solve my problem…I just want him to listen to me (and be empathetic and supporting)." But he typically replies (being the analytical problem solver that he was trained to be): "If you have a problem, solve it by step 1, 2, 3…otherwise, don't whine about it!" The reader may think that this is exaggerated, but it's not. However, this same dialogue repeats itself time and again and is also made by the spouses of other occupational group partners that tend to emphasize analytical skills rather than or more than interpersonal skills. From this clinical experience, an overarching theme that surfaces is lack of active listening skills and an inability to maintain emotional intimacy. This type of intimacy is frequently used only when a goal is in mind, and is disregarded the rest of the time. The bottom line here is that listening and observing before speaking (or determining a course of action) is a must. It is possible that in some of these instances, a degree of narcissism enters in and can make things worse — a sense of "I can't understand why they feel that way…I don't." In the new corporate era, management will not work using the command-and-control tactics of the past. This new era calls for adeptness in interpersonal relationships, especially empathy. The manager will have to behave more like a coach, using empathy and other interpersonal skills to get the best out of their subordinates, *versus* commanding them to give their best irregardless of how they feel about it. In today's knowledge-based companies, it is not possible to *demand* that workers give us the creativity necessary to develop the next breakthrough product that will be the next corporate cash cow? One of the reasons that we see so many of the most talented workers leaving companies for others (going out on their own) is probably related to how they were treated. It is said that one of the biggest lies of our time is, "People are our greatest asset." It's time we act as if we mean it when we say it.

Potential Opportunities Associated with Average Levels of Empathy:

The opportunities to improve in this area are many. Improvement in this area begins with our general attitude we have towards other people. In the work world, people aren't obstacles to be run over in our quest to get what we want. Empathy involves stepping outside of our box and getting in theirs for a bit...to think the way they think and feel the way they feel. Learning to see situations from these different angles helps us to learn more and is a powerful strategic planning tactic. Skillful use in this allows us to make better decisions and to deal with them proactively up front. Individuals and organizations with low levels of empathy can't see the forest for the trees. They fail to assess the impact of a decision on others, especially the customer, and tend to have a myopic view that excludes the power that other's feedback can provide.

Learning to be more empathetic takes practice, and we all have the potential for improving this skill. We can begin by simply asking ourselves a few basic questions. When relating with others, we must first ask: "How might the other person interpret this event...what meaning will they likely assign to my actions...what belief will they form about it?" Let's consider the following example of a boss who is a poor communicator. He decides to forego the required feedback sessions with his employees because "they know how I feel" and "they'll know when they have made a mistake." Exercising a bit more empathy, the boss should first realize that people are not mind readers. They can't really know how he feels about their performance unless he tells them, which in essence justifies giving them feedback in the first place. A more empathetic approach would also require the boss to try to anticipate how his employees might have interpreted his decision not to give them feedback. This could range from "he doesn't care about us or appreciate what we do" to "it doesn't matter to him what we do...so, whatever we do is okay with him." If the boss was more empathetic, he might realize that these are not the conclusions that he would like for them to make. Another question that we must ask ourselves is, "What feelings might others have about a certain event?" The feelings we experience about certain events are largely driven by the meaning we assign to them. In our example, some employees may feel angry noting that "the boss doesn't care," and others may feel somewhat sad that "he doesn't appreciate what we do," while others may feel happy that "whatever I do is okay with him." Finally, we have to ask, "What behaviors might result from these feelings?" Once again using the above example, it might look like this:

1. Belief   = "He doesn't care and doesn't appreciate all our hard work."
2. Feeling   = Anger.
3. Behavior = "I'll show him...I'll purposely corrupt this computer file and then we'll see how he likes that!"

The whole idea from this example is to understand that if we fail to realize that people assign different meanings to events and that these meanings drive certain feelings, which will in turn drive certain behaviors, we run the risk of tactically failing to anticipate the firestorm that our actions sometimes set off. We now have to go one step further. Since we aren't mind readers, we have to verify our impressions or hunches by actually talking to people directly: "It appears that you are angry about my decision not to provide regular feedback to you." The more we do this, the better we get at it.

A skill closely related to empathy is the ability to use our senses before we act. This is clearly observed in animals that have keener senses than humans, which they use instinctively to read situations; these enhanced senses, in turn, drive their behavior, which is often very intelligent. For example, because dogs can sense when a person is going to have a seizure, they have been trained to alert epileptics of seizures shortly before they occur so that their owners can sit down to avoid falling and hurting themselves. There are many other examples in which animals take time to read situations by using their senses and then act in such way that can actually be considered *emotionally intelligent*. In our rush to act, we seldom take time to read the situation before we act.

Failing to read cues and respond appropriately can lead to disastrous results in our work and professional life. Even in the animal world this is born out. In one instance, primate scientists were studying a gorilla that had been raised since birth alone, isolated from other gorillas. This particular female gorilla was first exposed to another female and then to her infant. This interaction went fairly well. Then, both females were allowed to enter the territory of a male gorilla. The two females stayed somewhat distant from the male at first (which was the thing to do). However, the female who had grown up not being around other gorillas was not skilled in picking up normal social cues. She didn't recognize the importance of observing personal space, male dominance, and acceptable social behavior. She scurried over to the male and pushed him. This [provoked] an attack from the male, which resulted in his grabbing and throwing the young female down a concrete moat and nearly killing her. This exemplifies that we have to sit and observe situations before we can act, especially in unfamiliar circumstances. This again involves using our senses, which are described below:

(1) **Vision:** Many of the cues we need to read from others can be visibly seen. Two areas consist of facial expressions and body language. Although this takes practice, some of the basics can be learned quite easily. Once again, failure to read these cues often leads to difficulty in interpersonal relationships. Reading facial expressions is easier if the person is not purposely trying to hide or disguise their emotions. From facial expressions, we can pick up a lot of important information about what people are thinking or feeling. Start with the area around the eyes. A raised brow can denote surprise, and it can also mean that the person knows the answer to what they are asking rhetorically. A lowered brow can signify that the person is confused, perplexed, or thinking. This can be a cue to clarify further what we've said or restate. The eyes themselves have been called the "windows to the soul." Does the person look directly in your eyes or away? Looking directly denotes a sense of openness — nothing to hide. Looking away can signify dominance — the boss looks directly into the subordinate's eyes, and the subordinate looks away. It can also mean that the

person is trying to conceal or hide something or that they are uncomfortable. Pupils sometimes restrict briefly when people get angry. The lips are also revealing. When people get angry, the lips, and sometimes the jaw muscles, tighten. Smiles are different based on the circumstance. For example, a smile of genuine enjoyment usually involves crinkling of the muscles around the eyes, but a polite social smile usually involves only the lips. Learning to read faces begins with simple observation like watching peoples' faces as they talk and trying to figure out what they are feeling from facial expressions. One excellent way to practice and hone this skill is to watch a video, preferably of a drama, with the sound off for a few minutes. Take notes trying to identify specific cues and what feelings or emotions you see the actors trying portray. Then, play back the tape with the sound, and see how accurate your observations were. For those who get good at this, a more advanced technique is to watch a foreign language film with subtitles. Even when observing people from a different culture, we can pick up on some basic emotions.

(2) **Body Language**: Body language has been the subject of numerous research studies and books. Observing body language has frequently been referred to as picking up on the nonverbals. The idea here is to assess congruence between spoken and non-spoken language. For example, what does it mean to hear a person say they are not angry while their fists are clinched and their jaw muscles are tightened? Examining this type of incongruent behavior is one of the better ways to practice picking up on the nonverbals. You can start by just trying to notice the changes you see in a person from one encounter to another. A normally cheerful person who suddenly looks annoyed or who distances herself or himself is probably upset about something. Body language includes posture, direction of gaze, length of gaze, smiles, stance, distance or proximity, hand motions, the position of the arms, and so forth. Some of the more basic cues to concern oneself with are length of gaze, especially when first meeting someone. Prolonged eye contact signals disapproval or hostility, or perhaps a wish for greater intimacy.

On the other hand, not making eye contact can signal dishonesty or deceit. Stance is generally a problem for some people. Women tend to be more comfortable face to face, while men prefer a side-on that becomes more frontal. Additionally, to remain standing while others are sitting transmits dominance. Standing with hands on hip or doing a lot of finger pointing communicates a sense of sternness. Sitting with arms high across chest can communicate the same or perhaps a sense of "I don't believe you" or "I'm not open to what you are saying." Proximity was illustrated from the previous example of the gorillas. We tend to feel aroused, uncomfortable, or threatened when someone violates our space. These "comfort zones" vary with culture and gender, so it's quite easy to send an unintentional message. For example, in Saudi Arabia, men prefer a comfort zone of 18 to 30 inches while Americans and Europeans prefer 30 to 48 inches. The idea is to learn to respect other people's preferred proximity, and not to invade their space unless you want to increase their anxiety. The idea here is that we have to try to consider what all these signals are telling us as a whole, versus isolating ourselves (and not tuning into the nonverbals) or reading too much into just one signal.

(3) **Listening:** Many of us could immediately improve our empathy by listening more than we speak. Some of us are so anxious to speak and respond that we fail to actively listen to what people are really saying. Listening involves looking for inflection, tone of voice, intensity, and rate of speech just to name a few. Additionally, we might want to listen for sequencing, flow, and emphasis in speech. Again, one of the best ways to practice is to observe others' interactions. It's interesting to watch the dynamics of staff meetings — from the basics of noticing who sits next to whom, to verbal and nonverbal communication, and to the effect of the communication that's transmitted. In such situations, it's interesting to observe who is more skilled in using empathy to pick up on these cues and adjust on the fly and who is not. Psychotherapists have long emphasized the importance of active listening especially when working with couples, families, and

groups. The idea is that one must sit quietly and listen...really tune in to what the other person is saying, then attempt to repeat the true meaning (not just a parroted playback) of what was being said. This then allows the other person the chance to validate (or invalidate) the accuracy of your perception, which allows you to clarify it even further. This is a fairly easy exercise. People are often surprised at how out of touch they are with understanding the feelings of the spouse they have known for many years. Once again, listening, when combined with other senses, is a powerful tool to help us read the cues in order to more accurately tune in to others and determine a better course of action with them. It's often helpful to get away to a quiet, peaceful spot, preferably in a natural setting, and just practice using our senses. What do you hear? What are the subtle noises? What do you see? What do you smell? What do you feel? Some of us have spent so many years in the concrete jungle that we have grown apart from some of our own natural senses. If you've ever spent any time in a wilderness setting, you'll understand its basic value just by practicing this simple technique.

Lastly, empathy also means allowing your intuition or your heart to be a factor in what you do. That constitutes listening to that still small voice within us; to ignore it can lead to terrible mistakes at times. That voice may say "don't," but we refuse to hear it, only to have to apologize later for our actions. Some people seem to be more intuitive or better at allowing their heart to guide their actions, but we can all improve this skill at least to some degree. This is one of the areas that society is thought to be moving further and further away from. The idea is that we are capable, with ever increasing ease, to act in an ever increasing disregard for the feelings or consequences that our actions might have on others. This kind of thinking has allowed mankind to perpetrate untold atrocities on others that serve the true interests of no one. Underlying this is a sense of selfishness that seeks self-gratification at whatever the expense. Today's team-based organizational cultures can not tolerate this type of behavior, and we are seeing that this behavior by management towards employees has backfired. Today, people want to work for employers who not only treat them with respect and have a "heart," but also for those who do what's right towards the environment and the larger society as a whole. We are seeing more and more organizations promoting a spirit of volunteerism among employees and even allowing them some time to give something back to the community. The idea we must grasp from this is that it is possible to be successful in a business sense and also do the right thing for people, the environment, and the greater society as a whole. The key to this is that it's not necessarily the easy road or most popular to take, but it is the one that leads to a sense of right behavior that will be a strength in the years to come, instead of being perceived as a weakness. What may seem to be prosperous and lucrative for a time, when it doesn't consider the greater good of others, will ultimately lead to failure.

Threats Associated with Very Low Levels of Empathy:

As previously alluded to, the threat for the individual and for the organization of not being sufficiently empathetic is that we will miss important social cues that frequently can lead to disastrous results. This inability to read and pick up on these cues, most specifically the emotions of others, isolates us from valuable feedback necessary to make on-the-fly adjustments in our long-term plans and in our immediate actions. It dooms us to a course of action that, once launched, we seem to doggedly stick with regardless of the impact and are surprised later when it ultimately doesn't work. If we could have understood what the cues or signals along the way were telling us, we could have used them to modify our approach and ultimately arrive at a more successful outcome. It's sad to witness the fact that every given day, entire companies operate with a sense of profound deficit in this area that places them so out of touch with what's going on around them that one has to wonder "who's asleep at the wheel here?" This emotional nearsightedness and tone deafness can propel us down paths fraught with personal and business casualties that should make us ashamed rather than proud of our actions. There are those that feel that achieving the ultimate goal is worth the damage we do along the way and that success comes at the expense of others ("So what's the big deal?"). That very way of thinking is the threat. That view looks to only the present and fails to grasp the wisdom in the saying that "success or fame is fleeting." Then what? Who do we turn to when our world falls down around us and after we've alienated people along the way? What good will we have done to gain success only to share it alone or at the expense of our family or friends?

Corporately, what value is there in making a product and then ignoring its impact on others, which may lead to paying out large sums of revenues earned in consumer lawsuits?

Greed and selfishness produce their own end. It will eventually take you to a place where you don't want to go, keep you there longer than you want to stay, and make you pay a far greater price than you want to pay. The question is *what will it take for us to see that?* Some are bound for a hard lesson.

Bottom Line Suggestions for Improving Empathy

"Personal Remedies":

- How do you feel when someone shows concern for you, and how does it make you feel when you show an interest in others?
- Actively show more concern for those around you, and try to see how that affects them, how they react to it, and how it makes you feel in return.
- Try to see the situation from the other person's perspective.
- Make an effort to be more sensitive to others' feelings, and try to understand how other people are feeling. Tune in more to the nonverbals.
- Try to increase your ability to understand how other people are feeling and why.

This will help you relate better with others.

- When you have an encounter with someone less fortunate than you, try to understand how it feels to be in that position.
- The next time you notice someone smiling, try asking why he or she

is feeling so good.

- When you come in contact with someone who appears to need assistance, ask if there is something that you can do.
- If you see someone who looks a bit confused or lost, try to be of assistance.
- The next time you see someone crying, try to understand what happened and ask if there is something that you can do.

"Group Remedies":

- Encourage people at work to tune into others more, to take more of an interest in their coworkers, and to ask them how they are feeling.
- Set an example by asking how your coworkers and subordinates are getting along from time to time.
- Encourage others to see how they can help if they think someone is having a bad day.
- Make a list of birthdays and anniversaries of the people you work with, and surprise them by celebrating these special days at work.
- Try "job shadowing," where you spend a day or more with someone else in order to better understand that person's work and responsibilities.
- Organize a group at work, or perhaps a retreat, in which you can discuss the importance of empathy and how to improve this skill.
- Explain what is meant by empathy and why it's important for one's overall ability to successfully cope with daily demand.
- Emphasize why improving this skill will have an overall positive effect on the productivity of the organization as a whole.
- Point out that empathy is extremely important when working with others, when relating to people, and especially when working in teams.
- Tell them that being empathic conveys a good feeling at work — it shows that you care about people.
- In smaller groups, have one member try to express an emotion nonverbally (by facial expression and body language), and have the others try to understand what that person is feeling.

Social Responsibility

Social responsibility is the ability to demonstrate oneself as a cooperative, contributing and constructive member of one's social group. This ability involves acting in a socially responsible manner, even though it may not benefit one personally. Socially responsible people have social consciousness and a basic concern for others, which is often manifested by taking on community-oriented responsibilities. This component of emotional and social intelligence relates to the ability to do things for and with others, accepting others, acting in accordance with one's conscience, and upholding social rules. These people possess basic interpersonal sensitivity and are able to accept others and use their talents for the good of the collective, not just the self. This aspect of social awareness has to do with accountability, integrity, trustworthiness, cooperation, and collaboration, which are vital for organizational activities such as team building and negotiation; these are all considered to be important managerial competencies by the US Office of Personnel Management (Corts & Gowing, 1992).

Strengths Associated with High Levels of Social Responsibility:

High levels of social responsibility identify individuals who are cooperative, contributing and constructive members of their social groups; these people are often described as responsible and dependable. This factor surfaces as significantly important for people involved in general sales, insurance, and employment counseling. Strength in this area also is requisite for the team-based culture that currently characterizes much of the knowledge work being done today, and will be even more important in the future. This skill equates to a sense of selflessness, or *esprit de corps*, that implies a sense of obligation towards one's social group members. It also implies a strong sense of self-other integration and trust. Based on experience with military units in combat, group cohesiveness, which is characterized by a high sense of social responsibility towards one's buddies, is one of the most potent defenses against combat stress. Emile Durkheim, the French sociologist, noted that one's ability to cope with life's difficulties is related to the degree one is integrated and regulated by his or her social group or culture. A fine line exists between a nominally integrated loner to being overly integrated, altruistic, and willing to give one's very life. These individuals typically like helping others and avoid exploiting or taking advantage of people. Others frequently depend on them. These people genuinely seem to care about what happens to others. They respect others and their feelings, and they typically don't like to see others suffer. Finally, socially responsible people are usually characterized as law-abiding citizens who avoid breaking the law even if they could get away with it. This skill is foundational for good family relationships, marital relationships, and being a productive and contributing member in one's community and work life.

This concept is a two-way street on an organizational level. Companies that expect a sense of social responsibility from their workforce, but who don't reciprocate, will frequently be the losers in the competition for workers in the knowledge economy. Several recent studies have indicated that workers care about the organization's responsibility towards the workforce, the environment, and greater society as a whole.

Weaknesses Associated with Low Levels of Social Responsibility:

People who have a weak sense of social responsibility may entertain asocial or even antisocial attitudes, take advantage of others and act abusively towards them, and may possibly have problems controlling their anger from time to time. Weakness in this area can mean potential difficulty in teamwork. Weakness here denotes a sense of greater concern for self and personal gain rather than concern and care for others. Individuals with weakness in this area are often seen as difficult to count on and are typically known for not helping others or showing concern for what happens to other people. They are typically disrespectful towards the feelings of others and may even exploit or take advantage of others for their own gain. In severe instances, they may even have a total disregard for being law-abiding citizens, perhaps choosing to break the law for personal gain, especially when they feel they can get away with it.

Weakness in this area on an organizational level denotes a degree of mistrust and lack of group cohesiveness with an attitude of "every man for himself." It will become increasingly difficult for organizations weak in this area to establish and compete in a team-based culture, as well as participating in alliances with other organizations necessary to establish oneself in the global corporate ecosystem of the future.

Potential Opportunities Associated with Average Levels of Social Responsibility:

One of the first ways to improve this skill is to stop shifting the blame for our problems onto something or someone other than ourselves. It means beginning to be more accountable and responsible for our behavior. We can't expect others, whether they be our children or coworkers, to be responsible when we don't act in a responsible way. Instead of the typical "I can't," we should more honestly say, "I don't want to" (or "I have to" or "I want to" do something else). The idea is that when we relate with others dishonestly, we are implying that someone other than ourselves is making us do something or preventing us from doing something. Many times, this is the easy way out — continuing to lay the blame elsewhere, and thereby carrying on in a less than responsible manner. Society today does little to seriously promote a sense of connection with and responsibility to something larger than ourselves. The trend towards isolation in our homes, or "cocooning," works against social integration into one's community, culture, or workplace. A good way to get out of this is to volunteer. Whether it be through schools, religious groups, community programs, or in one's workplace, there are ample opportunities to volunteer. Once we begin to do volunteer work, we come to realize that we are part of something bigger than our own small circle of family and friends, and we become more aware of and begin to understand the plight of others that share this planet with us. Additionally, choosing to be more responsible in this way represents an active orientation towards life in general rather than placing blame on someone else.

Those who are responsible in a business sense not only meet the standards of acceptable and moral behavior, but they typically avoid limiting themselves to only doing the assigned tasks; they look for other ways to contribute outside the parameters of their mere job descriptions. When these types of people see things that need to be rectified, they do something about it — they attempt to fix it, versus declaring that "it's not my job." This comes with a sense of an appropriate evaluation of what aspects of these situations we can control and how best to act, followed by letting go of the rest that we can't really control. This works against a swing towards the other direction, of being overly responsible and taking responsibility for things that are not ours to take, which actually facilitates others to be irresponsible. This type of behavior frequently meets a need in some people's lives — to be caretakers and to feel needed. Moreover, the focus on other's problems can be a way to avoid dealing with our own problems.

Taking responsibility for ourselves doesn't give us a green light to justify the means by the end. We should begin with respect for others and admit that they don't exist just to serve our needs. We are not entitled to exploit or treat others as if they were a means to our own ends, nor should we take their contributions for granted. Obviously, the idea is that we frequently have goals or encounter situations that require cooperation and participation from others. Additionally, others have to see an incentive for a win-win, or a *quid pro quo*. Our goal then becomes to offer them the incentives that are meaningful to their needs and interests, and allow them to also benefit. This goes against Darwinian logic of "only the strong survive...survival of the fittest...I got mine, now you have to get yours...there are winners and losers in the world, and you lose." This logic can justify any means to the end, regardless of the carnage we leave along the way — victory at all costs!

Nathaniel Branden, author of *Six Pillars of Self Esteem*, espouses the use of a sentence completion test that is designed to increase responsibility:

- If I operate with 5 percent more self-responsibility at work, I will...
- If I operate with 5 percent more self-responsibility in my relationships, I will...
- If I accept full responsibility for my own happiness, I will...

Branden suggests writing six to ten endings for each of the sentences over a two-week period in order to encourage a more responsible approach to dealing with one's life.

Threats Associated with Very Low Levels of Social Responsibility:

The ultimate threat in this area is antisocial behavior. The threat is based on the genuine disregard and lack of concern for others and their feelings — everything is justified in the conquest of personal needs and in the quest of self-satisfaction. This paves the way for total disregard for the rights of others and potentially breaking the law. In a sense, this breeds situational ethics and lack of morality. For example, a response to the question of whether it's right or wrong to steal might be: "Well, I don't really care if it's right or wrong…because what determines if I do it or not will be the chances of getting caught and the consequences." In other words, if the reward is great enough and outweighs the considerations, it's worth it stealing. This narcissistic and psychopathic view towards life breeds a cavalier attitude that will lead to one's eventual downfall. Organizationally, the threat is ultimate loss of our *raison d'être* (reason to exist). Ultimately, no one will be served by this type of behavior — not our long-term goals to succeed as a company, nor our employees, nor our customers when we operate with significant deficits in this area. Corporate history is replete with the fast buck failures that exploited others for temporary gain. Today's companies will do well to avoid the moral quagmire that this sort of behavior breeds and to steer towards a more responsible approach to doing business.

Bottom Line Suggestions for Improving Social Responsibility

"Personal Remedies":

- Think how you feel when you do something irresponsible and the way people typically react to that. On the other hand, how do others relate to you when you act responsibly?
- In addition to thinking how various situations influence you, try to think how these situations affect others — put yourself in their shoes.
- Think of something nice you can do for someone else, and do it.
- Try to be more involved in your family and at work.
- Make an effort to cooperate more with others around the house and at work.
- Do more at home, before being asked.
- Taking on more responsibility in your community.

- Try doing something beyond the limits of your usual task at work. Take on a project that others will benefit from.
- Think about what you can do to improve your neighborhood, and make a plan.
- Volunteer for something in your community or neighborhood.

"Group Remedies":

- Encourage coworkers and subordinates to contribute more to the group.
- Try to build an atmosphere of togetherness, of group cause, of working towards common goals, and of creating something that is important that everyone is part of it.
- Encourage others to take more responsibility at work and to ask what they can do to help before being asked.
- Discuss the long-term goals of the organization and how everyone can contribute.
- Try to stress that the group is involved in constructive goals that contribute to the good of society in the end (in some form or another).
- Organize a group at work, or perhaps a retreat, in which you can discuss social responsibility and ways to improve it in the workplace.
- Explain what is meant by social responsibility and why it's important.
- Emphasize why improving this social skill will have an overall positive effect on the productivity of the organization as a whole.
- Convey that the social cohesion of the organization as a whole depends upon the degree of social responsibility of each and every member.
- Tell the group that responsible, positive, and contributing employees typically receive more responsibility at work and are frequently promoted to managerial and leadership roles.
- Have them discuss various ways that they can demonstrate more responsibility at work, concern for their fellow coworkers, and things that they can do for the good of the group as a whole.

Interpersonal Relationship

Interpersonal relationship involves the ability to establish and maintain mutually satisfying relationships that are characterized by emotional closeness, intimacy, and by giving and receiving affection. Mutual satisfaction includes meaningful social interchanges that are potentially rewarding and enjoyable. Positive interpersonal relationship is characterized by the ability to give and receive warmth and affection and convey intimacy to another human being. This component of emotional and social intelligence is not only associated with desirability of cultivating friendly relations with others, but with the ability to feel at ease and comfortable in such relations and to possess positive expectations concerning social encounters. This social skill requires a general sensitivity towards others. This factor is essential for important managerial competencies like building bonds in the workplace.

Strengths Associated with High Levels of Interpersonal Relationship:

Individuals with high levels of this social skill are able to establish and maintain mutually satisfying relationships. These people have capacity for intimacy and the ability to give and receive affection. They are group-oriented, demonstrate social participation, and are often described as extroverts. Our research has clearly demonstrated that interpersonal relationship is a requisite skill for those involved in sales, marketing, management, customer relations, and those who work in the "people" professions like employment counselors and psychologists. Strength in this area is also a valuable skill for the team-based culture that will characterize the era of intellectual capital. Individuals with high levels of interpersonal relationship are able to show affection, can share deep feelings with others, are fairly cheerful and fun to be with. They tend to have good relations with others, tend to maintain close friendships as well as maintain a broad-based social network, and are generally considered to be "sociable" by others. Some of these individuals have the quality that gives others the confidence to confide in them. This skill is a critical foundation to good marital and family relations, and is essential for successfully navigating the ecosystem that will characterize the corporate world of the near future. Individuals high in this area are frequently the "go to" people that get involved in critical negotiations and in "fence-mending" endeavors. It's interesting to note that in many companies, if the CEO is weak in this area, they tend to have a No. 2 person who is strong in this very important social skill, who frequently goes behind smoothing over the ruffled feathers and putting out the fires that the CEO creates. This is a valuable skill in many ways and is essential for team-based activities and skillful leadership.

Weaknesses Associated with Low Levels of Interpersonal Relationship:

Difficulty in establishing and maintaining interpersonal contact is often related to an inability to express warmth, shyness, feelings of uneasiness around others, and a lack interpersonal sensitivity. In more extreme instances, this is associated with misanthropic attitudes and a basic distrust of others as well as a general suspiciousness of their motives. Weakness in this area limits people in social and occupational relations. Many of these people choose occupations that tend to isolate them and do not require significant interaction with others due to previous difficulties earlier in life in interpersonal relations. Early in life, if one has difficulty with establishing peer relations, a natural tendency is often to socially withdraw. One of the earliest ways we learn the ropes in this area is taking part in activities that require group- or team-based interaction, such as sports, scouts, band, and so forth. The idea is that if at first we don't succeed, "try and try again." Many of the lessons necessary for effective social behavior are learned in these groups, such as turn taking, cooperation, conflict resolution, working together for the good of the whole, and how to deal with failure. Again, our natural instincts are to withdraw if we have difficulty here, which in fact is one of the worse things that we can do in terms of our overall development. Unfortunately, today's world does little to encourage the development of this skill. Individuals often choose to "nest" in the solace of their own home. You can order in food, shop by telephone or the internet, do your banking by computer, chat virtually, spend hours entertaining yourself playing video games or web surfing, and even have "phone sex." Unfortunately, this does little to teach one how to interact in a meaningful, mutually satisfying manner with others, let alone be a "team player." In our interpersonal relationships, lack of skill here diminishes the ability to maintain *emotional* intimacy with significant others. In marriages, this is often cited indirectly as one of the reasons couples divorce. They frequently note that they married because they "fell in love" and they divorced because they "fell out of love." What happened between falling in and later falling out of love? Many cite a gradual decline in intimacy, specifically emotional intimacy. When we explore this even further, many times the only intimacy they really ever had was physical. The story has an obvious punch line to it: if it's only based on sex, then it's difficult to maintain over a longer period of time because the physical aspects can come and go. It's little wonder that many today choose to have relationships with others at the same time they are in a relationship. We have espoused a *throw-away* style that leads many down a trail of multiple relationships strewn with casualties of convenience. It's easy to maintain surface level relationships under the influence of the novel or the physical attraction, but, as the Eagle's song asks, what will we do "when the thrill is gone." It's usually when relationships move beyond the surface towards the substance of emotional intimacy that many become uncomfortable and leave; it's the same with social relationships at work as well. Individuals with low levels of interpersonal relationship may have many surface level relationships, but few of true substance. Often this comes from difficulty in sharing feelings with others and from being unable to give or receive affection. Wives frequently note this weakness in their spouse, noting that he has no difficulty with affection when there is a conquest in mind; but outside the bedroom, they have no need for it. Another aspect of this is the *male myth* that men don't show feelings or the *family myth* that "the Smith women are strong and don't let this stuff bother them" or "we don't tell them that we love them because they know it." It's sad that when we have children, we tend to pass this nonsense down to the next generation. This is especially true in alcoholic homes. Family members learn to deny their feelings, pretend that nothing is wrong, and stuff it all inside. Many children born into these families, go around hurting as young children, wanting affection and someone to pay attention to them. Since many of the alcoholic parents are emotionally anesthetized, the child soon figures it out. "I have two choices here: (1) I can go around hurting because no one seems to care, and I can't take this dysfunctional mess; or (2) I won't let them hurt me because I won't have feelings, and since I have no feelings, they can't hurt me." This then becomes the intergenerational madness, and we teach the same behavior to our children through our actions that we used to hate as a child.

Potential Opportunities Associated with Average Levels of Interpersonal Relationship:

The opportunity to improve this area should be seized for the reward is truly great. The ability to enjoy deep and meaningful relationships with others provides a foundation for stability and growth as well as a source of satisfaction in life.

Andrew Dubrin, author of *Magnetism: Discover Your Own Charisma and Learn to Charm, Inspire and Influence Others*, refers to the ability to attract the respect and adoration of others as "personal magnetism," which he describes as a captivating and near charismatic quality. Based on seven years of studying people who truly possess this quality, he notes several characteristics worthy of review in order to gain some ideas on how to relate better with others:

- They are emotionally expressive and say how they feel enthusiastically. They are open, positive, and constructive.
- They communicate extra-verbally as well as verbally. This means that they make good eye contact, smile, are warm, stand straight to radiate confidence and magnetism, keep their arms open, and use enthusiastic hand gestures.
- They are able to flatter others and appear realistic and sincere when they do so. Their compliments are individualized rather than general or vague. These people are also good listeners, which is another powerful form of flattery conveying that the other person is worth listening to, and they quote the other person showing that they have paid attention to the conversation.
- They have a well-developed sense of humor. This is important because we like to be around people who make us feel good. It is important to stress that their type of humor is not sarcastic, harmful, or at the expense others — the important difference here is that they laugh with people and not at them. Their humor is typically based on simple everyday life situations and is spontaneous. These people also know how to laugh at themselves, which shows inner strength and

self-confidence if it's not done as a form of self-deprecation.

- These people show genuine concern for people. They take an interest in the health and well-being of others. Empathy and sincere caring has a powerful effect. These people are typically considerate and think about the impact of their comments on others. They give others credit for their ideas and express gratitude for receiving them. Considerate behavior doesn't mean you're weak, rather it's a way of demonstrating respect.

Larry King, of CNN's *Larry King Live,* has interviewed over 30,000 people including many famous celebrities. His book, *How to Talk to Anyone, Anytime, Anywhere: The Secrets of Good Conversation*, offers some basic conversation secrets important for improving interpersonal relationship:

- Break the ice with a warm topic. The old tactic of opening with a cliché is a terrific conversation starter. Things such as the weather, movies, pets, sports, and children are generally safe starters.
- If you're shy, say so. Nothing beats honesty when you're trying to break the ice. King relates an example from his own life. In 1957, when he first began as a disc jockey, he told his listeners, "This is my first day, and I'm nervous" and "If anything goes wrong, please forgive me." In a social setting, you can show that you're human by admitting that big parties are overwhelming for you.
- Pick up the pace by asking open-ended questions. One of King's favorites is simply "Why?" People like to expound on choices they've made — like why they chose the profession they did — but be careful not to ask it in a judgmental way. Use "What do you think?" to ask people their opinions and impressions. "What if" is a hypothetical question that works well to perk up people's interest, especially, when speaking to several people.
- Show sincere interest. Listen while someone is talking instead of planning what you are going to say next (which is rude and causes you to miss important information). King notes that he never met a good conversationalist who wasn't a good listener; he summarizes this by saying "I've never learned much while I was talking."
- Develop a broad outlook. Don't just talk about yourself, and rarely use the word "I".

- Don't judge others in advance. This shuts down your curiosity and prevents you from learning something.
- End a conversation gracefully. Breaking away from a conversation is often more difficult than starting one. Leave a great impression when ending a conversation; end by making an excuse in a polite, friendly, and apologetic way — then leave.

Benjamin Franklin developed a system of self-improvement principles to fine-tune his behavior, which he called the "Art of Virtue." He outlined these in his autobiography that was published in 1771 in the hope that it would inspire and teach others. Michael Loren authored a book titled *The Road to Virtue: Resolutions for Daily Living Inspired by the Wisdom of Ben Franklin.* Loren summarized Franklin's basic points, some of which have applicability here for improving interpersonal relationship. He points out that Franklin was a good listener. He wrote that true knowledge was gained "by the use of ears rather than the tongue." He was noted to give others time for what they had to say, pausing to make sure they were finished, which in turn allowed him to hear more and learn. Franklin suggested to speak little and do much. He was aware that words were cheap and tried not to make promises he couldn't keep. He also recommended not to speak until your anger has subsided. Franklin was a sincere person and wasn't afraid of correcting himself. He also monitored what he said and chose the right time to say it. He noted, "Think innocently and justly, and if you speak, speak accordingly." Franklin was known for his friendship and was famous for helping friends rather than taking from them. He also kept in touch with his friends and was a prolific letter writer and a dedicated respondent — all before the advent of modern mail, the telephone, fax, and e-mail. He maintained confidences and offered to "protect your and other persons' peace and reputations." Finally, Franklin was modest, largely from the deep-seated belief that he was beholden to his community, neighbors, and family. He focused on being less argumentative, less openly critical, and didn't blow his own horn.

Threats Associated with Very Low Levels of Interpersonal Relationship:

The threat of significant weaknesses in this area stems directly from the fact that this skill allows us to successfully navigate the wide social spectrum from personal to work relationships. Profound weakness in this area tends to isolate people and causes "friction" that generates resistance from others, complicating our ability to successfully interact with people. Severe weaknesses in this area pose a serious threat for organizations, because there are few organizations that can tolerate a profound deficit in their ability to successfully interact with people. This can be a death-blow to companies that focus heavily on relationships with consumers and strategic partners. As previously mentioned, the new corporate world will rely on relationship webs and broad-based ecosystems; and one of the primary skills requisite to navigating the web and the ecosystem will be interpersonal skills.

Bottom Line Suggestions for Improving Interpersonal Relationship

"Personal Remedies":

- Ask yourself how it makes you feel when you're not that involved socially and how you feel when you're more socially active?
- Try to be more sociable and socialize more — people like and are attracted to sociable people. Think about ways that you can meet people, what you can do with others, and do them. Do something with other people at least once a week.
- Socially avail yourself to others more, and spend more time with people in general. Try not to refuse when invited over to someone's home. Don't make excuses, just go.
- Talk more with people, even if it is a bit artificial in the beginning. Show interest in others — listen to their stories, impressions, and points of view.
- Don't stay at home. Make an effort of going out more and meeting people. The next time that you're in a social gathering, don't sit by yourself, mix with others. Make more of an effort to introduce yourself to people you don't know. Try to get closer to those you like being with.
- Decide if you enjoy small social get-togethers or big ones, and then plan something at your house — invite the people you like and those

you think would like to be together.

- Make an effort not to let friendships get cold. Try contacting old friends or acquaintances that you haven't seen in a while.
- If you share a common interest with someone else, take the initiative to do something together.
- Think about someone you wanted to meet or to get closer to, and put a plan together of how to go about it. Then simply do it.
- Don't give up if someone is not interested in making or renewing contact with you; if it doesn't work out, just try socializing or being sociable with others.

"Group Remedies":

- Set up a system that introduces new employees into your organization. Select appropriate coworkers who can act as "immediate first friends and companions" who will show new employees around and introduce them to the people with whom they will be working.
- Encourage more group interaction and try to improve interpersonal communication at work. Think of ways that can create a nice social atmosphere at work. Help make the workplace a place where people like to be and spend much of the day.
- Build teams based on people who enjoy being and working together and who complement one another with respect to emotional and social skills.
- Organize parties and social get-togethers. Celebrate birthday parties, and organize family days and outings.
- Encourage employees to keep contact with coworkers who have moved to other departments or who have even left the organization altogether.
- Organize a group at work, or perhaps a retreat, in which you can discuss interpersonal relationship and how to improve it in the workplace.
- Explain what is meant by interpersonal relationship and why it's important for one's overall ability to successfully cope with daily demands.
- Emphasize the importance of interpersonal skills in the workplace

where people work with people, which demands relating well with one another.

- Emphasize that improving this skill will have an overall positive effect on the productivity of the organization as a whole.
- Get a discussion going in which each member describes how they feel they typically relate with others. Have them identify their weaker areas in social interactions.
- Have them discuss ways of improving their interpersonal skills at work.

PART 3:
Adaptability

Adaptability comprises a combination of *reality testing*, *flexibility*, and *problem solving*. One's general level of adaptability reveals how successfully one is able to cope with environmental demands by effectively "sizing up" and flexibly dealing with problematic situations. Being able to efficiently cope with organizational change requires adaptability. High levels of adaptability identify people who are realistic and effective in understanding problems, flexible, and competent at arriving at adequate solutions. Enhanced levels of adaptability indicate people who can easily find good ways of dealing with everyday difficulties. Not only is adaptability a valuable attribute in and of itself for daily living and normal functioning, but people who possess high levels of this attribute can make a substantial contribution in the workplace. These people might do well in research and development as well as in technical support departments. Moreover, our findings demonstrate that adaptability is a significantly important attribute in professions like engineering, nursing, and medicine.

Reality Testing

Reality testing is the ability to assess the correspondence between what is emotionally experienced and what objectively exists. Testing the degree of correspondence between what one subjectively experiences and what actually exists involves a search for objective evidence to validate and confirm feelings, perceptions, and thoughts. Reality testing involves "tuning in" to the immediate situation, attempting to keep things in the correct perspective, and experiencing things as they really are without excessive fantasizing or daydreaming about them. The emphasis is on pragmatism, objectivity, the adequacy of one's perception, and authenticating one's ideas and thoughts. An important aspect of this factor is the degree of perceptual clarity evident when trying to assess and cope with situations; it involves the ability to concentrate and focus when examining ways of coping with situations that arise. Reality testing is associated with a lack of withdrawal from the outside world, a tuning in to the immediate situation, and lucidity and clarity in perception and thought processes. In simple terms, reality testing is the ability to accurately size up the immediate situation. Reality testing is an important factor in conflict resolution and negotiation, which are considered to be very important managerial competencies by the US Office of Personnel Management (Corts & Gowing, 1992; Gregory & Park, 1992).

Strengths Associated with High Levels of Reality Testing:

High levels of reality testing are possessed by individuals who are able to evaluate the correspondence between what they experience (the subjective) and what in reality exists (the objective). These people are often described as realistic, well grounded, and tuned in to their environment. Their general approach in life involves actively examining rather than passively or naively assuming. They are usually good at sizing up the situation at hand. These individuals see things as they are without fantasizing or daydreaming about them and don't get carried away with their imagination or fantasies. They maintain focus and avoid fading out and losing contact with what is happening around them, even when upset. They avoid exaggeration and are able to keep things in their right perspective; they can tune into the reality of the immediate situation quite easily. It is interesting to note that reality testing is one the most significantly important factors possessed by successful engineers based on our research.

Strength in this area is critical for good problem solving and being able to accurately determine the situation at hand and the course of action to take. It is essential for strategic planning and can be a source of strength for organizations that are skilled in this area. Reality testing is about seeing things as they really are, even when the news is not good.

Weaknesses Associated with Low Levels of Reality Testing:

Weakness in this area indicates difficulty with tuning into and remaining focused on the problem at hand. It can contribute to faulty problem solving in the sense that it compromises accuracy in problem definition. Some individuals with weakness in this area tend to excessively daydream or fantasize. These people tend to exaggerate and get carried away with their imagination or fantasies, and some may have difficulty pulling out of daydreams, returning to the reality of the immediate situation, and maintaining the right perspective. They may tend to fade out, and some may even lose contact with what happens around them. Inaccurate perceptions, illogical thinking, and inappropriate emotional reactions with little or no attempt at validating them is indicative of poor reality testing.

Weakness in this area can surface as critical organizational flaws that may eventually threaten the existence of the organization as a whole. This type of weakness can seriously hinder the organization's ability to interact with competitors by interfering with its capability of receiving, interpreting, and using feedback to determine an appropriate course of action in dealing with problematic situations. If this skill is underdeveloped and inefficient, the results become obvious. It's like trying to use a compass with a magnet attached to it — the readings would obviously be incorrect and obscure the real direction that one must follow in order to find the proper path that will lead one out of the forest. Companies that have significant flaws in this area are characterized by successive misfires, work-rework, duplication, waste, and a sense of being out of touch with customers and the need to change. Persistent weaknesses in this area can lead to continual poor returns on investment and eventual decline. This skill will become even more critical in the future, when the ability to accurately interact with a constantly changing environment will be mandatory for peak performance. Weaknesses in reality testing have led to the downfall of leaders, entire companies, and nations — simply because they were unable to see things as they really were. Those who do possess good reality testing and try to save the sinking ship are often the victims of the ancient custom of *shooting the messenger of bad tidings.*

Potential Opportunities Associated with Average Levels of Reality Testing:

Improving reality testing begins with gaining better perceptual clarity...seeing things as they really are, versus how we want them to be. In an effort to sharpen our perceptual clarity we have to stop and take stock of where we are, and evaluate what we are doing and what we have accomplished. This should be an ongoing process that is done on a daily basis. But what exactly should we be taking stock of? What we should be taking stock of is how successful we are in meeting our goals. What goals? As individuals and as organizations we set goals that we wish to accomplish. These goals should first be realistic and obtainable within an equally realistic time frame. The degree to which we have accomplished these goals determines how successful we are. Perceptual clarity and reality testing come into play in both the setting of our goals and in evaluating how successful we are in accomplishing those goals.

There must be a threefold approach towards success through (a) maintaining a balance between *personal* and *family* life on the one hand and *work* on the other, and by (b) balancing the *body-mind-soul* model. Success skewed in the direction of one's occupation at the expense of the family resulting in poor health and spiritual emptiness is not success. We should also be taking stock of this approach to defining success as an opportunity to improve our reality testing and ability to keep things in their proper perspective.

If we discover that we are heading in the wrong direction and are out touch with objective reality in any of the above areas, we should pause and reflect. The purpose of this is to break the cycle, the self-defeating mind sets, and the denial that serves us all too well in order to put things back in their proper perspective. Try to identify the illogical thoughts and ineffective behaviors involved in what we're doing. This helps us pinpoint the specifics of our faulty thinking so that we can reevaluate our behavior and get back on track.

The object of pausing and looking at what we are doing and why is to improve perceptual clarity and, in turn, reality testing. This helps us begin to question and seek evidence to confirm the way we are presently assessing things — "Who says it's so...where's the proof...where's it written...is their evidence to confirm my assessment?" To be effective in doing this, we have to conquer our fear. This fear is what drives our denial (of seeing things the way they really are), fear that if we or others see us as we really are, they might not like us, they may pass judgment, or in some way hold us responsible. We have learned from a very early age to deny and do what it takes to preserve self which, at times, runs the risk of preventing us from reaching the truth about ourselves as well as the world around us. It takes far more courage to step from behind this elaborate system of filters that work to color and distort reality in a manner consistent with the way we want it. Additionally, it takes courage once we see where we are wrong, to do something about it.

An additional way we can improve our reality testing is to develop a close network of honest confidants and mentors — the kind of people who can tell us we're wrong when we are. It is said that *people surround themselves with what their ears want to hear.* It's easy to surround ourselves with people who will blow in our ear and make us feel good. But what good does that really serve? We have to ask ourselves if we have the courage to hear the unpopular voice. This difficulty becomes even more profound in many large organizations in which the senior leadership has distanced itself from objective reality by believing what they want to believe. Such situations make one wonder who's really steering the ship. Some of the more enterprising CEOs and senior managers frequently immerse themselves outside their subjective corporate reality into the reality of the workforce...often on the factory floor with the workers themselves. Other executives hold regular meetings with a broad cross-section of the workforce including the most junior workers. This improves reality testing because the vision of these junior employees hasn't yet become clouded by the biases and faulty beliefs of the corporate culture.

Threats Associated with Very Low Levels of Reality Testing:

One of the most serious threats associated with poor reality testing is the deleterious effect it has on problem solving. Poor reality testing makes it difficult, if not impossible, to accurately tune into the problem at hand, define it correctly, and come up with and implement appropriate solutions. When both reality testing and problem solving are thrown out of action, it is impossible to adapt, perform and function effectively as an individual and as an organization. Individuals and organizations alike begin to lose focus, proper perspective, and the ability to make decisions. This increases the possibility of other threats and often leads to a final death-blow that shuts down the system. The road back to recovery is extremely difficult if not impossible.

Bottom Line Suggestions for Improving Reality Testing

"Personal Remedies":

- It's easier to cope with things if you *examine* the immediate situation rather than jumping to conclusions.
- *Tune* into the immediate situation, and put things in their correct perspective.
- *Search* for objective evidence to support what you are feeling and thinking when sizing up the situation.
- *Test* the correspondence between what you experience and what objectively exists.
- Spend more time *checking out* how accurate your feelings, thoughts, and ideas really are, rather than relying too heavily on your gut feelings.
- Concentrate and focus more on the obvious when *examining* various ways of coping with situations that arise.
- When you're developing an opinion about something or somebody, *collect* more outside information to see if that's the way it really is.
- *Talk* about your ideas and feeling to others to get their feedback.

Sharing your feelings and thoughts with others may help you gain more objective insights.

- The next time you think someone feels a certain way about you, *ask* others what they think.
- Rather than reacting automatically, *stop and check* the situation out to see if your actions are really justified (based on evidence).

"Group Remedies":

- Organizational goals should be clear, realistic, and attainable.
- Emphasize information-sharing among employees.
- Encourage people to talk to one another and exchange ideas. Discourage working alone.
- Encourage people to ask questions at work and discuss various issues related to work.
- Encourage open communication, and stress the importance of giving and receiving feedback.
- Require your subordinates to check out their ideas with you and with coworkers.
- Discourage behavior and activity that is based on jumping to hasty conclusions and assuming, rather than on examining the facts.
- Organize a group at work, or perhaps a retreat, in which you can discuss reality testing and how to improve the areas that need to be improved.
- Explain what is *reality testing* and why it's important for one's overall ability to successfully cope with daily demands.
- Emphasize why improving this skill will have a positive effect on the productivity of the organization as a whole.
- Have them discuss what difficulties they might have in this area and ways they might improve it.

Flexibility

Flexibility is the ability to adjust one's emotions, thoughts, and behavior to changing situations and conditions. This component of emotional, personal, and social intelligence refers to one's overall ability to adapt to unfamiliar, unpredictable, and dynamically changing circumstances. Flexible people are agile, synergistic, and capable of reacting to change without rigidity. These people are able to change their minds when evidence suggests that they are mistaken. They generally are open to and tolerant of different ideas, orientations, ways and practices. Flexibility is considered to be one of the most important managerial competencies by the US Office of Personnel Management (Corts & Gowing, 1992; Gregory & Park, 1992). This factor also plays an important part in other managerial competencies like conflict resolution and negotiation.

Strengths Associated with High Levels of Flexibility:

Individuals who are highly flexible have an enhanced ability to adjust their emotions, thoughts, and behaviors to changing situations and conditions. They don't experience difficulty beginning new things or making adjustments in general. They can change their opinions about things, can make changes in their daily life, and can change old habits as well. They typically can adjust to new conditions and are resilient. We have found in our research that flexibility is a significantly important factor for people who are successful in marketing. This trait is an essential trait for corporate survival in the era of intellectual capital, the knowledge worker, and the digital revolution. We are already seeing that nothing is static and that constant, at times rapid, change will be the norm. Obviously, those who are flexible and are good in dealing with change will fare much better in these times. Cast against flexibility is the old mind set of security. Many companies are now seeking workers with an entrepreneurial mind set and are using flexible pay systems (such as stock options and pay for performance, and so forth) to find those willing to take risks and grow with the company, versus show up for the security of the same job and a steady check. Even in Asian countries, where near lifelong jobs were an enshrined institution, we are seeing this erode as companies face survival in the global corporate ecosystem. Rigidity in responding to the fluid nature of our times will all but end a company's chances to evolve and survive. Thus, a corporate strength required to deal with these changes is precisely flexibility. This skill also contributes to problem solving and stress tolerance and is aided by high levels of optimism. Today, and even more so in the future, individuals and companies will be required to make fast, on-the-fly changes, scanning and digesting feedback from their environment and adjusting accordingly. To be able to do this, one has to have a certain ability to take risks, conquer the fear of the unknown, live with a certain degree of uncertainty, and change direction or opinions when evidence suggests that we are mistaken. Strength in this area also suggests an ability to be open to and tolerant of different ideas, orientations, ways, and practices.

Weaknesses Associated with Low Levels of Flexibility:

Weakness in this area implies rigidity and lack of openness to change. People who are not flexible exhibit rigidity in their thinking and behavior. They tend to resist change in general and are against change in themselves in particular. Weaknesses in this area indicate difficulty in making adjustments in general, beginning new things, changing opinions, adjusting to new or unfamiliar situations, changing old habits, and making changes in daily life. Perhaps for many, underlying this, is a need for the security of the familiar and a certain sense of uneasiness about the unknown. Weakness in this area does not serve one well today in the modern corporate era, and this will certainly be the case in the future, which will be characterized by constant and ever increasing change. Individuals and organizations with weakness in this area will experience difficulty in changing their views and goals when the need to do so will arise. This desire or need to cling to one's opinions, even in the face of contrary evidence, suggests rigidity and perhaps fear or maybe even narcissism in some cases ("I am right and they are wrong...they are the one's who have to change"). Consequently, weaknesses in this area make individuals and organizations resistant to new ideas and intolerant of different opinions or practices. Individually and organizationally, there has to be a certain degree of permeability in our boundaries in order to receive, digest, and process input from our environment. Rigid and impermeable boundaries wall off individuals and organizations, creating isolationist views that don't evolve when necessary. In the end, this can result in going the way of the dinosaurs for failure to survive environmental changes. With respect to this potential flaw, note how many senior corporate personnel are not information-smart. Many of these people avoid or *rigidly* resist e-mail, don't use the internet, don't like corporate "chat" areas on the intranet, and have little time for the so-called "propeller heads" who do. The problem is that the lack of even the most rudimentary savvy here will only widen the schism between the organization and its customers. The requisite skill is to be able to roll with the punches and channel and harness change flexibly as a catalyst instead of trying to throw water on it. Persistent weakness in this area will have a deleterious effect on developing high-performing teams and organizations — one of the salient traits that characterize such groups is precisely the ability to deal with change.

Potential Opportunities Associated with Average Levels of Flexibility:

Improving flexibility will yield handsome results on the individual and on the organizational level. Many people resist change by sticking to what is secure and comfortable for them, and they tend to become overwhelmed by change rather than adjust and adapt to it. Therefore, one of the rudiments in dealing with the uncertainty and fear of rapid change is to first develop a sense of inner stability — knowing who you are, what you stand for, what your values are, and what purpose you have in life. This goes a long way in reducing the anxiety we experience in facing the uncertainty of our times…the peace and calm that comes from being grounded from within. Many seek to manage their anxiety by *self-medication*, whether it be in the form of alcohol, drugs, or some other unhealthy and self-destructive substance or practice — the idea is to mute the tenor of one's life circumstances in hopes of being able to deal with it. Unfortunately, this doesn't work. One reality that we must deal with is our own irrational thoughts, like expectations of stability. This sets us up for the inevitable letdown when this expectation is not met. Another faulty expectation involves risk and uncertainty. In these turbulent times, the reality is that everyone is at risk — individuals, marriages, and organizations. The ability to deal with this risk will be a key survival tactic. One way of dealing with it is to try to stay informed in the era of information overload. Some see the immensity of this task and simply give up. Information that we receive and process can provide us with an important aid in our attempts to adapt and evolve when necessary. Another reality that we must deal with is the stress that frequently accompanies change. We would be well served to pursue techniques to manage stress like aerobics, meditation, relaxation exercises, or stress-reduction techniques. Such activities will provide us with a healthy balance between physical, mental, and spiritual health; this, in turn, will help us to be flexible enough to face change and challenge. Networking is another tactic that builds in a support system to deal with change…to help us see it coming and evolve with it.

Truly successful people seem to thrive on change or to proactively use it to their benefit. They appear to be constantly seeking ways to improve themselves and are quick to see the opportunities that accompany change that others dismiss. On the other hand, many of us resist change because we prefer the comfortable environments we try to create for ourselves and the roles and rituals that accompany them. Change creates a sense of anxiety, which is an uncomfortable feeling viewed as threatening our stability. Rather than experience the potential loss that frequently accompanies change, we dig our heals in and resist it, which is a defense mechanism aimed at reducing the anxiety.

Once again, in order to become more flexible, the journey begins from within. Start by clearly defining your goals…what you want to achieve in your personal life and at work.

A sense of purpose that provides vision goes a long way in helping us transcend the difficulties associated with change. This implies developing a sense of who you are.

In addition to an internal set of values that provide a compass with which to navigate the waters of change, the second area we must work on is our attitude. We must begin by ruling out quitting as an option. Starting by developing a will to persevere in spite of the situation is like building an internal engine that powers us to do what we have to do to cope. The idea here is to improvise, adapt, and overcome, as if that were our only option. A frequently heard comment from individuals facing potential change is, "I can't." However, seldom is this true…that we can't manage the change. This should be rephrased to "I don't want to," "It's not important enough to me," or "I'm not willing to pay the price." We have to move from viewing change as the enemy to accepting it as an opportunity for growth.

Last, we have to have the intellectual integrity and courage to see things as they are, versus how we want them to be or would like them to continue to be. Few people today have the courage to do this because it involves admitting when we are wrong, taking responsibility, making amends, changing, and moving on. It's far easier to rationalize, deny, project blame, avoid responsibility, tell ourselves again that "we're right and they're wrong," and stay the same as we are.

Threats Associated with Very Low Levels of Flexibility:

The ultimate threat of significant deficits in this area is decay and death. Rigidity becomes the rigor mortis that sets in and ensures the loss of mobility and the ability to evolve, and then we go the way of the dinosaurs, becoming fossilized and watching the world from inside of a museum rather than actively participating in life itself. Rigidity also creates a sense of emptiness...as if that which made us truly alive has departed. To survive and thrive, we have to be flexible and evolve as part of a complex ecosystem of mutually dependent organisms, all necessary for each other's long-term survival. Remaining rigid does not allow us to be a part of this ecosystem, but rather isolates us from the world around us. We must maintain permeable external boundaries to allow for the fresh intake of growth nutrients and the purging of materials that have ceased to contribute to our development.

Bottom Line Suggestions for Improving Flexibility

"Personal Remedies":

- Don't be afraid of change. Try to react to change without stiffening up your back or turning up your nose — just accept it...as an opportunity to learn new things and grow.
- Think of different ways in which you could handle the same situation, do the same thing, and approach the same problem or challenge.

- Watch other TV programs that you don't or wouldn't usually watch.
- Take an interest in another ethnic or cultural group other than your own, and try to learn more about them.
- Try speaking with more flow without thinking that much about your words or the order or structure of what you want to say — just talk.
- Rearrange or change the furniture in your house. Try experimenting with different styles and colors.
- Try a different hairstyle or choose a different style of dress.
- Visit a place that you have never seen before. Do it without planning — just get up, go, and enjoy the adventure of it.
- Relax your daily routines. For example, alter something in your morning ritual from the time you wake up until the time you leave the house — try mildly changing the set hour that you generally wake up and leave the house, the way brush your teeth, wash, select your clothes, dress, eat your breakfast, and so on.
- Try making decisions quicker than you usually do — simplify and speed up the process a bit, and use more gut-level guesswork.

"Group Remedies":

- Encourage openness and flexibility at work, and discourage rigidity and being closed to different approaches.
- Encourage dialogue between people who typically hold very different ideas at work.
- Stress that change is natural in all organizations and that it is very important to be ready to change with the changing situations that arise. Convey that change can be positive and important for progress if the organization is to move forward.
- Discuss the importance of open-mindedness and flexibility before anticipated organizational change.
- Encourage and reward creative ideas for coping with everyday problems that arise at work.
- Give a personal example by being more open and flexible.
- Continuously think of how best to introduce new and more efficient systems at work.
- Organize a group at work, or perhaps a retreat, in which you can discuss

flexibility and how to improve the areas that need to be improved.

- Explain what is flexibility and why it's important for one's overall ability to successfully cope with daily demands.
- Stress that improving this skill will have an overall positive effect on the productivity of the organization as a whole.
- Have group members ask one another how easy or difficult it is for them to be open to new and different ideas, people, and situations in general.

Problem Solving

Problem solving is, essentially, the ability to identify and define problems as well as to generate and implement potentially effective solutions. Problem solving is multiphasic and includes the ability to go through the following process:

- Being *aware* that a problem exists and needs to be dealt with
- Being *motivated* enough to deal with it
- *Defining* what the problem is
- *Generating* potentially effective solutions
- *Deciding* on one of the solutions
- *Implementing* the potential solution

Being aware that a problem exists is, basically, being able to identify problems when they occur — being able to see it coming and determine that certain situations are problematic. Not all such situations are seen or dealt with immediately. The individual has to be concerned and motivated enough to deal with it. Some problems are dealt with at a later time, and others are never dealt with at all. Some people establish a type of priority as to when certain problems should be dealt with if at all — which one is more important to deal with first, and so on. If a person is motivated and concerned enough to find a solution to a problematic situation, there is typically an attempt to define and formulate that problem as clearly as possible. This stage includes collecting information about the problem itself — how it began, how serious is it, how it affects me, how this type of problem has been solved in the past, and so forth. The next step is to generate potentially effective solutions, which is like brainstorming. The person has to then weigh the pros and cons of each possible solution, and choose the best course of action taking into consideration everything that the person knows about the problem. Finally, the last stage is to go ahead and implement the selected course of action to solving the problem at hand.

This skill is also linked to a desire to do one's best and to confront problems, rather than avoid them. Problem solving is considered to be one of the most important managerial competencies by the US Office of Personnel Management (Corts & Gowing, 1992; Gregory & Park, 1992). Together with reality testing and flexibility, problem solving plays a very important role in other important managerial competencies like the ability to negotiate and resolve conflicts.

Strengths Associated with High Levels of Problem Solving:

Good problem solvers are adept at quickly recognizing and defining problems; these people attempt to solve problems rather than avoid them. They characteristically push forward and deploy some sort of method of overcoming difficulties. They try to get an overview of the problem before trying to solve by collecting as much information as possible. They typically try to think of as many approaches as they can for dealing with it and look at each possibility. Once this is done, they generally don't have difficulty in deciding upon a good solution and implementing it. These people are often systematic and demonstrate disciplined perseverance on the one hand and spontaneity in solution selection on the other. However, there are good problem solvers who do not methodically go through all of the above-mentioned phases in an organized manner, but they do come up with solutions that work. The more creative problem solvers are able to come up with more potentially effective solutions than others.

Strength in this area is a true asset, both individually and organizationally. This skill is especially critical for effective strategic planning; it is essential in anticipating and dealing with potentially complex problems on a large scale. This is especially necessary for individuals working alone, or with minimal supervision, who typically have to deal with situations as they arise without the benefit of group decision making. Our research findings have demonstrated that this skill is significantly important in identifying successful engineers, teachers, and social workers. This is a requisite skill for the operations side of many organizations, especially critical for those situations that have to be worked *on the fly*. Strength in this area is vital for multidimensional thinking, the capability to maintain and visualize many complex issues in working memory, and the ability to conduct cost-benefit analyses in one's head. This skill is requisite for systems thinking, especially in anticipating the interaction and effect certain actions have on others, and locating points of leverage for maximum effect with the least expenditure of energy and resources as possible.

Weaknesses Associated with Low Levels of Problem Solving:

Weakness in this area can indicate a tendency to get "stuck" when thinking about different ways of solving problems, difficulty deciding on the best solution, and difficulty in utilizing a multi-dimensional approach to analyze and solve problems. Some individuals with weakness in this area may lean towards a more impulsive, gut-instinct approach, without logical analysis of possible consequences. Difficulty in this area could indicate difficulty with understanding cause-and-effect relationships, and anticipating logical outcomes for certain actions. This difficulty may be accompanied with difficulty in impulse control and reality testing. In the more severe cases, some individuals demonstrate serious thought disturbances. Some individuals or organizations may almost view an impulsive, shoot-from-the-hip style as a strength, viewing that ability to act quickly on instincts to not miss an opportunity is preferred in today's business culture. Interesting conceptualization, but this is exactly the point. Sacrificing accuracy for speed will cause many individuals or organizations to overlook opportunities or solutions they might have seen, or avoid consequences that could have been anticipated, if a more effective problem solving approach had been utilized. Weakness in this area organizationally represents significant cost in terms of the work-rework that accompanies ineffective solutions to problems.

Potential Opportunities Associated with Average Levels of Problem Solving:

There are a number of methods that can be used to improve problem solving, some of which are quite straightforward and easy to master. One such method is as follows:

1. **Exploration** — What is the problem? Who's problem is it? How do you define it?
2. **Assessment** —What are all the possible solutions to this problem? List pros and cons for each. Which seems to be the best solution based upon a cost-benefit business case analysis?
3. **Goal Setting** — Define the goals in specific, behavioral, measurable terms. Who is responsible for each part? What are the time lines? What are the deliverables? What are the specific methodologies and resources needed ?
4. **Implementation** — Set in motion the results of step #3.
5. **Reevaluation** — Did we accomplish our desired outcomes? If not, why not? What adjustments can be made to achieve better results? Do we need to use another method, or stick with our present approach?

An even simpler approach to improving this skill is called the "Seven P's": Proper Prior Planning Prevents Pitiful Poor Performance! In spite of its lack of sophistication, this approach simply emphasizes the importance setting up an organized plan of attack — and how effective we are in doing that has a lot to do with the quality of the outcome.

Another interesting approach involves the use of imagination. Such an approach was employed by Dr. Jonas Salk, the eminent immunologist who discovered the polio vaccine. When he observed certain phenomena in the laboratory that he didn't understand, he would ask himself: "Why would I do that if I were a virus or a cancer cell in the immune system?" (*Bottom Line Personal,* August 1, 1995). This type of approach to problem solving helps us *think outside the box.*

The key skill that many individuals and corporations need to remain competitive is the ability to innovate, which is a form of creative problem solving. Innovators are keen observers, have a restless curiosity, ask questions, are able to identify things that others miss, have a talent for generating a large number of ideas, see things in new ways, and seem to routinely question the status quo. Innovators and creative problem solvers have the ability to think big and build a tolerance for bad ideas. These people have amazing resilience to deal with countless rejections. Another factor that tends to spur creativity and can exploit multidimensional problem-solving skills is diversity. Many of the major breakthroughs within certain fields have come from contributions from outside those fields. This points to the importance of seeking out diverse companions. By associating and working with people from other disciplines, a cross-pollination of ideas can occur — people gain from learning how other people approach problems. Many of the great thinkers and problem solvers read broadly, not just within their chosen area.

Captain Scott O'Grady, the US Air Force pilot whose F-16 was shot down over Bosnia in 1995, demonstrated real world problem-solving skills that directly led to his safety and recovery by pararescue personnel. He co-authored *Return with Honor* in which he offers some excellent tips to solving problems based on his experience:

- Take control of your mind before fear sets in. The idea here is to think rationally and avoid *emotional hijacking* that can short-circuit effective solution finding.
- Think about your training and what you already know about solving problems. Don't get emotional or try to cut corners. If you haven't received training related to your specific situation, think about how you handled similar situations.
- Get organized, clearly formulate the problem, think of ways of solving it, set priorities, and ask for help if you can.
- Be optimistic, and think positive. Negative thinking is a dead end. Focus on what's necessary to solve the problem.
- Don't dwell on mistakes you made while solving the problem. Preserve your self-confidence and your conviction that any obstacle can be overcome.
- Mentally prepare yourself for the long haul. Taking this type of view dilutes disappointment . when the solutions don't emerge immediately.
- Mentally motivate yourself. Contemplate what others have been through, which can help you put your own problems in perspective.
- Break the rules only when your goal is in reach. Only when success is in sight can you improvise, otherwise you run the risk of jeopardizing everything you have gained.

From a corporate perspective, poor problem solving can mean a death blow to the organization. Even though companies may hire the best people and spend large sums of money on training them and on research and development, many keep "blowing it." David Smith, head of knowledge development at Unilever, lists nine symptoms of *bad brainpower management* (Stewart, *Fortune,* June 23, 1997), which provide a number of ideas for improving problem solving:

1. **Mistakes get repeated** — Ralph Nader used to say that your best teacher is your last mistake. Companies that practice hiding their mistakes fail to learn from them and run the risk of litigation, which often results when companies continue to make the same mistakes. Obviously, the best way is to seriously analyze mistakes and learn from them. In the process of effective problem solving, an approach that doesn't work should be replaced by another potential solution to the problem that might work.

2. **Work gets duplicated** — The saying "don't reinvent the wheel" applies here. Companies fail to copy success equally as often as they fail to learn from their mistakes. Being organized and methodical in the problem solving process decreases the possibility of duplicating procedures and approaches, especially ones that don't produce results.

3. **Strained customer relations** — Customer complaints are typically related to the product, not understanding what they have been sold, or getting the run-around. The implications here are that customers provide an opportunity to learn, yet many companies fail to see it this way. Customer complaints provide a valuable source of feedback vital to the continued improvement of products and service. Good problem solvers learn from others and use what they've learned to come up with better solutions.

4. **Good ideas don't get shared** —This is perhaps one of the greatest problems of our time. Good ideas often do not transfer between departments, units, companies, and even countries. The way to solve this problem perplexes many. On the one hand we have to convince people to share ideas rather than hoard them, and on the other hand we have to prepare others to accept or at least be open to these ideas rather than reject them. Idea sharing is part of the information-gathering phase of problem solving

and depends upon good interpersonal communication, which in turn depends upon other important emotional and social skills like empathy, assertiveness, and flexibility. Developing creative ways to improve interpersonal communication and to share knowledge pays off in the end for companies. Tom Stewart offers some starting points for facilitating this process. He stresses the importance of setting an example — great bosses and great teachers who love teaching produce great students. This means sharing your ideas with others and being open to receiving ideas from others. He then suggests that the leader should begin to use the new ideas, which makes them more acceptable for subordinates. Stewart also recommends creating incentives. Many companies pay for performance, and this can be extended to how well personnel share and borrow ideas. Additionally, it's important to compare one unit's ability to share ideas with that of another unit and reward both for improvement. Many companies don't internally benchmark and, thus, suffer from spotty performance from within, promoting an attitude of every unit for itself. Lastly, Stewart emphasizes the importance of making this whole process fun.

5. **You have to compete on price** — A frequently repeated mistake is taking the customer for granted, especially long-standing customers, and failing to continue to learn and develop with them. This problem has probably caused the loss of many accounts for businesses. Here it's important to stress that the way out of the commodity business is knowledge, especially when company and customer learn together. The more we can learn about specific customer needs and preferences and the more we adjust to meet those expectations, the harder it becomes for would-be competitors to beat us out. Once again, all of this is important for improving overall problem solving on an organizational level.

6. **You can't keep up with market leaders** — Many feel that they can't compete because their competitors are so big and powerful. However, history is replete with Davids overtaking Goliaths because they studied their competitors, found out what the competitor knew that they didn't know, adjusted, and exploited this accordingly; this

relates to the problem-definition and information-gathering stages in good problem solving.

7. **You're dependent on key individuals** — Lew Platt, CEO of Hewlett Packard, points out that you have a "knowledge problem" when decisions are made too high in the organization. This indicates that people either lack the knowledge that would let them think and decide for themselves or they have been taught not to.

8. **You're slow to launch new products** — Fast companies will rule in the future of continuous change. Knowledge and the ability to solve problems quickly, accurately, and faster than anyone else is the strategy that will have to be exploited to guarantee success in the fast future. It is obvious that we are in a critical period of transition in the corporate world, moving from the wild west to the fast future; only those who fully grasp this point will survive.

9. **You don't know how to price for service** — The idea here is that if you don't know how to price for service or charge what you charge, it's admitting to your customers and competitors that you lack knowledge. However, it's important to stress that we will know who should pay for what if we simply understand that customers typically buy solutions to problems. Additionally, it's important to know that the more knowledge intensive a service is, the less it is open to outside threat and the greater the market value it has. There's not much of a premium for commodity knowledge.

Robert Sternberg, author of *Successful Intelligence: How Practical and Creative Intelligence Determine Success in Life*, has suggested that there are three basic components of successful intelligence that are directly related to problem solving: *analytical thinking* (the ability to solve problems and judge ideas), *practical thinking* (the ability to use your ideas and implement them effectively), and *creative thinking* (the ability to formulate new or clever solutions to problems). In discussing *analytical intelligence*, Sternberg lists six basic points than can be used to improve problem solving:

1. **Recognize that there is a problem** — This is an obvious, but overlooked, point. Avoidance, denial, or an inability to zoom in on

the immediate situation (poor reality testing) doesn't serve us well when we are faced with a problem.

2. **Define the problem** — Once again, this is an obvious point. The way we define the problem has a lot to do with the way in which we try to solve it, and inaccuracy in problem definition can cost time and money.

3. **Represent information about a problem accurately** — Nothing can substitute for accuracy in the world of fast companies. The ability to quickly and accurately size up a situation and act will be critical in gaining strategic advantage in first-to-market competition.

4. **Invest in resources** — It is important to think strategically when investing time and money in order to facilitate effective and successful problem solving.

5. **Allocate your resources wisely** — From a business standpoint, this includes doing a cost-benefit analysis, examining the potential risk and rate of return factor, and carefully selecting the strategies that produce the greatest leverage.

6. **Track your progress during the problem solving process** — The idea here is to learn from the process itself and your mistakes in order to select the best course of action accordingly.

Sternberg's *practical intelligence* is essentially about being able to translate the theoretical or abstract to "where the rubber meets the road." It is said that after management implements a new venture, some will ask, "Yes, it worked...but should it have worked in theory?" It is often a question of *just doing it*. In exploiting practical intelligence, we have to begin with our own business case analysis: *What are my strengths and weaknesses...what skills constitute my greatest points of leverage...where do I have the most traction?* The idea here is that practical thinking is about maximizing our true strengths and minimizing our weaknesses. We then can strengthen the skills in which we excel and find ways around those things we don't do so well. The key issue here is how effectively we cover all the bases. It's not about being the best at everything, it's about developing our core competencies, networking and aligning with others who offset our weaknesses to cover our soft underbelly where we frequently take the gut shots that can lead to our downfall. The strategy involves analyzing and finding these areas and then countering each with strengths from others so that we have the greatest potential for survival. Finally, there is no substitute for believing in ourselves. Failure is part of success, and if we tell ourselves we can't do it, it is more than likely that we won't. These self-fulfilling prophecies of doom and gloom have a lot to do with outcome; we would do well to seek to persevere rather than give up prematurely, learn from our mistakes, and modify our behavior along the way.

Sternberg's *creative intelligence* is, essentially, the ability to go beyond the usual solutions to generate new ideas and different ways of doing things. However, to go against and beyond the accepted ways of doing things often exacts a price, and one must have a strong ego to overcome potential barriers along the way to bringing about change. Lastly, in our quest for ways to enhance problem solving, it's helpful to reconsider older models like Socratic reasoning, which also emphasizes the questioning of assumptions. In almost every human endeavor that has lead to great change, it could not have been possible without those who questioned the prevailing assumptions, took risks, made mistakes, and allowed others to make mistakes in the process of creatively solving problems. Taking risks is an essential for creativity, but it's wise to take calculated risks and not foolish ones. Once again, a cost-benefit analysis is what's required here: Are we willing to pay the cost associated with the risk involved?

Threats Associated with Very Low Levels of Problem Solving:

The gravest threat associated with significant weaknesses in problem solving is the potential for catastrophic failure. A serious inability to solve problems effectively combined with poor reality testing, poor stress tolerance, and poor impulse control can make it extremely difficult for individuals to effectively deal with their environment and experience even a moderate degree of success. This is like discovering that one is in a mine field only after having stepped on a mine, and immediately forgetting that, stepping on another one. Perhaps, more than ever before, we are creating problems of greater complexity, magnitude, and frequency that make it increasingly difficult for mankind to deal with. Significant weaknesses in problem solving and in the overall adaptive response may, in a Darwinian sense, lead to the extinction of entire corporations who aren't able to solve the problems necessary to evolve, let alone survive. Those who survive, evolve, and prosper will be those who are able to effectively deal with and solve problems related to a complex and rapidly changing future.

Bottom Line Suggestions for Improving Problem Solving

"Personal Remedies":

- Be more aware of what needs to be dealt with in your daily life. Cope with problems that arise when they arise — don't avoid them or put them off.
- Prioritize the most important and pressing issues that need to be dealt with first.
- Try to define and clarify what exactly is the problem at hand.
- Get an overall picture of the problems that you deal with at home and at work — aim for both a panoramic photograph and an X-ray.
- Make an effort to see how the problem developed. See the way it's affecting you and others and why.
- When working on a problem, tell yourself that you can come up with an answer — there is a solution to most problems…you just have to work at it.
- Brainstorm as many solutions as you can to solve the problem at hand — the more options and possibilities you have to choose from, the better. Then, push yourself to generate additional and different ways of solving the same problem.
- Weigh the pros and cons of each possible solution, and then decide.
- Try to choose the solution that's best for you and the situation at that particular point in time.
- When you've decided on the best way of dealing with the problem, go ahead and do it. If it doesn't work, try another possible solution.

"Group Remedies":

- Create more opportunities at work to deal with problems together — organize problem solving groups and "hit teams" that wrestle with problematic situations as they arise.

- Encourage troubleshooting and dealing with problems rather than avoiding them.
- Emphasize the importance of defining, describing, and formulating problems as clearly as possible. Put the emphasis on getting the big picture and how it developed.
- Encourage and reward information gathering — collecting as much information as possible related to the problem at hand.
- Encourage brainstorming for potential solutions to problems.
- Convey the importance of weighing the pros and cons before deciding.
- Encourage and reward good decision making based on maximum information.
- Organize a group at work, or perhaps a retreat, in which you can discuss problem solving and how to improve it.
- Explain what is problem solving and why it's important for one's ability to successfully cope with daily demands.
- Emphasize why improving this skill will have an overall positive effect on the productivity of the organization as a whole.
- Walk them through some basic problem solving strategies, and stress that different approaches work differently for different people — they will have to find the technique that best suits them.

PART 4:
Stress Management

Stress management comprises *stress tolerance* and *impulse control*. Individuals with high levels of stress management are able to withstand stress without falling apart or losing control. They are generally calm, rarely impulsive, and work well under pressure. The ability to manage internal states, to regulate one's emotions, and to control one's impulses is important in conflict management at work. As such, these skills are very important managerial competencies. People who possess high levels of this attribute can handle tasks that are stressful or anxiety-provoking or even involve an element of danger. Stress management skills are critical for people who work on the *front line* like police officers, firefighters, emergency medical staff, social workers, and combat soldiers.

Stress Tolerance

Stress tolerance is the ability to withstand adverse events, stressful situations, and strong emotions without falling apart by actively and positively coping with stress. This emotional skill involves the ability to weather difficult situations without getting too overwhelmed. This ability is based on:

1. A capacity to choose various courses of actions for coping with stress — being resourceful and effective, being able to come up with suitable methods and knowing what to do and how to do it
2. An optimistic disposition toward new experiences and change in general and towards one's ability to successfully overcome the specific problem at hand — a belief in one's ability to face and handle these situations
3. A feeling that one can control or influence the stressful situation — keeping calm and maintaining control

This component of emotional intelligence is very similar to what has been referred to as *ego strength* and *positive coping*. Stress tolerance includes having a repertoire of suitable responses to stressful situations. It is associated with the capacity to be relaxed and composed and to calmly face difficulties without getting carried away by strong emotions. People who have good stress tolerance tend to face crises and problems rather than surrendering to the feelings of helplessness and hopelessness. The ability to efficiently manage internal states is an essential aspect of self-regulation, which is a very important managerial competency.

Strengths Associated with High Levels of Stress Tolerance:

High levels of this factor identify individuals who are able to withstand adverse events and stressful situations without falling apart. These people are generally able to cope with stress actively and positively. They are calm and rarely get overly anxious or agitated. They know how to deal with upsetting problems and believe they can stay on top of tough situations and handle stress without getting too nervous. They typically hold up well under stress, can usually control their anxiety, know how to remain calm in difficult situations, can deal with and face unpleasant situations, and believe in their ability to handle most upsetting problems. We have found in our research that stress tolerance is significantly important for being successful in marketing, selling insurance, and management. Strength in this area is a critical factor in dealing with the rapid and constant changes experienced in today's fast-moving corporate world. Strength in this area evokes a sense of confidence and quiet calm that one can handle what comes one's way. In a sense, it is the ability to know when and how to act proactively rather getting acted upon. People who are good at handling stress have a fair amount of self-discipline that allows them to stay on a task and see it through, in spite of the difficulty.

From studies on combat stress reaction and critical incident stress, several attributes have been shown to help survive these experiences. The first is confidence in one's self. This is the belief that one is capable and able to deal with difficult circumstances, no matter what they might be. Perhaps more than any other, the attitude one has towards oneself will determine the outcome of stressful situations. The second important attribute is confidence in one's training. This finding supports the saying, "We fight the way we train." Training apparently allows one to know how to deal with situations under optimal conditions. Additionally, this training should include how to recover from failures and suboptimal conditions. The third attribute is confidence in others. The ability to withstand stress is bolstered when we know that we're not in this thing alone — that others are there for us in these difficult situations. Last, confidence in our leadership is an additional attribute important for weathering very stressful situations. As part of an overall team, individuals can withstand significant stress in service to a goal when the leaders are envisioned as caring, competent, decisive, able to make right decisions, and have a clear sense of direction. Even though the ship may be in uncharted and turbulent waters, having a steady hand at the helm is apparently very important for relieving people's fears.

Weaknesses Associated with Low Levels of Stress Tolerance:

Anxiety appears when stress tolerance is not functioning adequately — it's a clear sign that this emotional skill is weak, inefficient, and simply not doing its job. Basic symptoms of anxiety then appear such as irritability, tension, disturbed sleep, poor concentration, and indecisiveness, which negatively affect one's ability to make decisions. These people typically experience a drop in self-confidence; and they tend to worry and appear somewhat fearful at times. As can be expected, these symptoms have an ill effect on one's overall ability to perform at work. In such a condition, many of these people find it more and more difficult to function at work. This condition often results in a drop in productivity.

Weakness in stress tolerance, from an organizational perspective, is often expressed by feelings of *burnout,* which are at times manifested by an increase in absenteeism, overuse of health care services, and even substance abuse as a form of self-medication. Additionally, weaknesses in this area can lead to significant health risk due to the effect that stress has on the body over a long period of time; there are a number of physical disorders that are related to stress and anxiety, a few of which can be life-threatening. Both directly and indirectly, anxiety is one of the major causes of loss of working days.

Potential Opportunities Associated with Average Levels of Stress Tolerance:

There are many techniques to choose from that can be used to improve stress tolerance. A great number of books have been written about managing stress, and the professional journals are replete with studies dealing with the effects of stress and stress-reduction strategies. It would be nearly impossible to do justice to this subject here in light of the enormous amount of material that has been published. We will, therefore, present a summary of some of the more well-known methods that can easily be employed to improve stress tolerance, especially on the job.

We react with feelings of fear, stress, and anxiety to what we perceive to be a threat. These feelings are triggered by the natural survival mechanism of *fight or flight*...alerting our body that we have to either fight off the threat or run for safety. We don't encounter real flesh-eating saber-toothed tigers anymore, which we have to fight or run from, but the effect of stress in doing battle with paper tigers can be just as tough.

The most common consequence of stress is cardiovascular damage like high blood pressure, heart attack, and stroke. Lack of control over one's job has been linked to higher rates of heart disease. A study of 7,400 British civil servants suggests that employees' autonomy on the job, regardless of their level of pay or responsibility, plays an important role in their health (*Wall Street Journal,* July 25, 1997). This study found that illness in the workplace, to some extent, is a management issue in that the way that work is organized appears to make an important contribution to the known link between socioeconomic status and heart attack risk. More specifically, those in low-grade positions with little control over their responsibilities were at a 50 percent higher risk of developing the symptoms of coronary heart disease than those in higher level jobs. The conclusion here was that giving individuals boring and repetitive work, that didn't make use of their skills, appeared to increase their risk of heart disease. The idea is that introducing more on-the-job flexibility and control pays off in more ways than one.

As was previously mentioned, there are several basic strategies that can be helpful in dealing with stress.

First, relaxation exercises are simple to master and can be very helpful. For example, Benson in *The Relaxation Response* suggests the following technique, which is perhaps the most widely used today:

- Sit comfortably with your eyes closed, and begin to relax your muscles.
- Breathe deeply placing your hand on your stomach just below your rib cage. As you breathe in, you should feel your hand rise.
- Silently focus on a word (Benson recommends "one") as you slowly exhale, or just focus on your breathing. Another variation of this step is to imagine a place or experience that produces positive feelings, and focus on this as you breathe. If you experience intrusive thoughts, just keep breathing deeply.

Benson recommends doing this exercise ten to twenty minutes once or twice a day; based on his experience, one should begin to feel calmer in dealing with stress. Additionally, this technique has proven helpful in dealing with hypertension, and painful medical conditions and procedures, as well as with chronic pain.

An additional approach shown to be effective in dealing with stress is aerobic exercise. It has been shown that programs that combine aerobic activity, such as walking, with some strength training provide a potent weapon in dealing with stress and maintaining good physical conditioning. It has been demonstrated that exercise has a positive effect on mood, acting as a natural antidepressant, and is also helpful in strengthening the body's immune system. The key to getting the best out of aerobic techniques is to exercise at least thirty minutes in duration no less than three times a week. Even moderate walking has been shown to produce beneficial effects.

Additionally, walking with a friend or spouse offers a great opportunity to talk and share without the distractions of home and work — and can help maintain more than just our bodies. It is important to point out that you should first check with your physician before starting any exercise program.

Another approach to enhancing our ability to cope with stress is better nutrition. A negative manifestation of modern life is eating quickly and an overindulgence in fast food establishments. Under peak periods of stress, loading our bodies with empty calories and pumping up on stimulants like caffeine and nicotine hype us up even more and defeat efforts to calm us down. The idea is to regulate fat intake and balance our diet with adequate amounts of fiber, protein, and carbohydrates. It's also important to hydrate — to drink lots of water. Water acts as a natural fuel and drinking approximately eight glasses a day has been recommended. Finally, many authorities have suggested using nutritional supplements like antioxidants (beta-carotene and vitamins C and E), selenium, and folic acid because of their purported effectiveness in fighting the wear and tear of life.

Sleep is another very important factor in reducing stress. Several studies have shown that Americans are working longer hours and getting less sleep. Fatigue is one of the common symptoms of stress, and we need at least seven to eight hours of sleep nightly especially during peak stress periods.

Close interpersonal relationships are considered by some to play an important role in stress tolerance. Several studies have demonstrated a positive health benefit from close relationships, especially healthy marital relationships. A number of studies have shown that married people are at lower risk for illness, accidents, and death than bachelors, divorcees, and widowers are. Even for the unmarried, having personal caring relationships with significant others helps in dealing with stress.

Spirituality is also considered by some to be an important factor in coping with stress. The late Dr. Robert Eliot, cardiologist and author of *From Stress to Strength: How to Lighten Your Load and Save Your Life*, emphasized the powerful effect of spirituality in reducing stress and stress-related physical disorders for some people. He discussed three "magic pills" — primary relationships, friendships, and spiritual support. Dr. Eliot argued that these "life ingredients" appear to have a significant effect in lowering the risk of various kinds of illness and accidents. His findings revealed that individuals reporting high levels of satisfaction in these three areas have one third fewer incidents of illness, accidents, and premature death than others. With regard to spiritual support, Dr. Eliot noted that research has shown that those reporting weak religious affiliations demonstrated mortality rates two to three times higher than those who reported strong affiliations. He understood this to mean that "forgiveness, understanding, and hope" are three very powerful means of reducing stress.

Threats Associated with Very Low Levels of Stress Tolerance:

The major threat associated with serious deficits in stress tolerance is the health-related risk factor, for individuals as well as for organizations. Heart attack claims about 520,000 people a year in the US making it a leading cause of death. This equates to one death almost every minute. Based on over thirty years of research, the previously mentioned Dr. Eliot concludes that heart attack occurs in part because of the way some individuals react to the rigors of daily stress. He pointed out that approximately one in five people have "surges in blood pressure to rival those expected in combat" in reaction to being exposed to the challenge of everyday activities and normal stressors. He referred to these individuals as "hot reactors" and concluded that stress-induced blood pressure surges, such as those experienced by these people, accurately predict coronary heart disease, heart attack, cardiac arrest, and stroke. He defines hot reactors as people who exhibit extreme cardiovascular arousal in response to standardized stress tests, which evoke dramatic and rapid increases in blood pressure. Stress for these people doesn't have to be earth-shattering. With regard to this observation, he concluded that "These walking time bombs burn a dollar's worth of energy for a dime's worth of trouble." The major danger here is that such rapid surges in catecholamines (stress-induced chemicals) can produce lesions within the muscle fibers of the heart; such catecholamine lesions are found in 86 percent of autopsies following sudden cardiac death. These catecholamine surges destroy thousands of cardiac cells within minutes according to Dr. Eliot. This violent response can be triggered by something as inconsequential as getting cut off in traffic. Hot reactors often appear outwardly calm — they are not the typical Type A cardiac patient. They are, however, particularly prone to perceiving loss of control and disappointments as a threat to their self-esteem and sense of identity; this, in turn, becomes a major health issue for them. Physical fitness programs have no real effect on hot reacting — these people continue to dramatically overreact to mild stressors irrespective if they exercise or not. Dr. Eliot also pointed out that there is an ever increasing number of women who are diagnosed as hot reactors each year. Lastly, in addition to the possibility of heart attack and sudden cardiac death, these people run the risk of other medical problems such as chronic hypertension, arteriosclerosis, accelerated blood clotting, kidney failure, and stroke.

From an organizational perspective, stress represents a major health hazard that has a significant impact on the corporate bottom line. Swedish researchers who conducted a long-term study at a Volvo plant found that when people work in an environment where they have a sense of fulfillment and accomplishment, they are more likely to remain healthy and productive. Steven Covey, author of *The Seven Habits of Highly Effective People*, refers to this as an "inside-out approach." The idea is that real organizational quality can only be achieved through developing personal quality, and the basis of organizational quality, productivity, and high performance is people...not assets or things. The point to be made here is that companies take care of the bottom line by taking care of their bottom line — their people.

Bottom Line Suggestions for Improving Stress Tolerance

"Personal Remedies":

- Be more aware of how you feel in stressful situations. Try to understand how these situations developed and what makes them so stressful for you.
- Believe in your ability to handle and successfully overcome these situations when they occur.
- Remember that these situations do not last forever, and there is always something you can do.

- Being optimistic is better for surviving difficult situations than being pessimistic or indifferent.
- Doing something when you're under pressure is better than doing nothing at all, and try to do a number of things.
- Divide larger tasks into smaller more manageable chunks, and concentrate on only those tasks that truly require your attention at the moment.
- Prioritize by identifying activities that can be delegated to someone else or perhaps left till later — spread these activities out, and don't let them pile up. Avoid leaving things to the last minute.
- When you feel stressed, breathe deeply, relax your muscles, remain focused, and speak slower.
- Fight the situation, don't give up. Stay on top of it, and do the best you can to overcome it.
- You have at least some control over difficult situations by trying to do something.

"Group Remedies":

- Try not to load up your subordinates with excessive work. Don't request from only a few — spread out the tasks and allocate responsibilities more evenly.
- From time to time, check to see how your subordinates and coworkers are holding up under pressure and see what you can do to lighten their load when necessary.
- Set an example, and pitch in and help especially when the going gets rough.
- Know when to ease up on people and pull back.
- Give more support to those who are most under pressure.
- Encourage people to slow down. Don't let the work pile up.
- When possible, make deadlines more flexible.
- Organize a group at work, or perhaps a retreat, in which you can discuss stress tolerance and how to improve the areas that need to be improved.
- Explain what is stress tolerance and why it's important for one's overall ability to successfully cope with daily demands.

- Emphasize why improving this skill will have an overall positive effect on the productivity of the organization as a whole.
- Walk them through a few basic stress reduction techniques — have them do one of the basic relaxation exercises.

Impulse Control

Impulse control is the ability to regulate one's emotions and to resist or delay an impulse, drive, or temptation to act. It entails a capacity for dealing with one's aggressive impulses, being composed, and controlling hostility and irresponsible behavior. Impulse control is basically self-control; together with stress tolerance, which is essentially one's ability to manage internal states, this emotional skill represents another important aspect of one's overall capacity for self-regulation. These factors are important managerial competencies that should seriously be considered when setting selection criteria, performance standards, and training curricula.

Strengths Associated with High Levels of Impulse Control:

High levels of the impulse control indicate individuals who are able to resist or delay impulses and defer drives and temptations to act. People with good impulse control rarely become impatient, overreact or lose control. They typically don't have bad tempers or difficulty controlling their anger. They are usually not loud, nor do they tend to over-talk — these people are in control of themselves and know when to speak and when to be quiet. They are not generally impatient, impulsive, nor do they have difficulty controlling their impulses; they rarely make foolish mistakes. Good impulse control is an essential in developing good problem solving skills and in negotiating successfully in difficult situations. Effective emotional control helps individuals avoid the temptation to act prematurely, and it aids in their ability to remain patient and wait for the right opportunity to maximize their success. Skill in this area also allows time to be empathetic and accurately read social cues, which provides us with valuable input needed to determine an appropriate course of action when dealing with people at work.

People with good impulse control are able to use *strategic waiting* as a power strategy to facilitate the fulfillment of goals. Our research findings have shown that good impulse control emerges as significantly important for successful engineers, clinical psychologists, psychiatrists, and social workers.

Weaknesses Associated with Low Levels of Impulse Control:

Weaknesses in impulse control can evidence themselves in low frustration tolerance, anger control problems, loss of self-control, and in explosive and unpredictable behavior at times. These people are often described as impulsive, hostile, aggressive, abusive, and irresponsible. Individuals with problems in this area may misstep due to acting too prematurely or are too quick to form an opinion about a situation, which may dismiss potential opportunities too quickly. Many individuals and companies don't see this as a weakness, believing that making "fast decisions" and reacting quickly to market forces are critical strategic skills to remain ahead of the power curve. However, the goal is to make quick accurate decisions, *not impulsive ones*, in order to maintain strategic advantage. A quick impulsive decision that involves rework is worse than a more deliberate but accurate move. Difficulties here can also lead to addictive behaviors, such as substance abuse, in some cases. Their behavior is often based on pure judgement and reckless thinking. Organizationally, this has a negative effect on problem solving and strategic planning opportunities. Being quick on the draw at the expense of accuracy equates to sloppy logic. Companies that have serious weaknesses in this area may experience significant costs associated with the misfires that accompany impulsive corporate behavior. Typically, many of these organizations are so focused on moving fast, reacting on instincts and "gut" impressions, that it is almost viewed as a company virtue. This frequently draws the fire away from the casualties of this style of operation — the costs of the wrong decisions. Companies that exercise this particular style of operation will frequently chalk these up as "the cost of doing business," which is justified with a "you win some...you lose some" mentality. They would do better to adopt a more deliberate and accurate problem solving and strategic planning style.

Potential Opportunities Associated with Average Levels of Impulse Control:

Improving impulse control begins with learning how to wait and be patient. It is important to balance your drive with *strategic waiting*. The idea here is to wait long enough to allow critical information to surface so you can make more accurate decisions. Patience serves us well for both collecting information as well as bouncing strategies off of others in order to receive their feedback before making decisions on how best to act. The importance of this point is stressed by the saying, "Haste makes waste."

Even if our gut instincts are usually correct, we should make an effort to pause before making decisions and acting upon them. Attune your ear to the small voice from within that whispers "wait." Such advice is important in one's personal life as well as at work. For example, some people are quick to get married only to later wonder, "Why they didn't see certain things in their relationship before they got married." In our relations with others, it's possible to pick up signs and signals from the other person that we might be trying to move things too quickly. Once again, this depends on our ability to take the time to look for these signs, which is similar to listening to the small voice within us. Even if we are so impatient not to pause long enough to pick up these signals, it should definitely be a sign for us to slow down when we note the reticence or anxiety that typically develops within time. The object then is not to rush a decision, but to slow up the process and more fully evaluate the situation. The idea here is to spend more time researching our decisions and submitting them to a *cost-benefit analysis*, so that we can say with some degree of certainty and confidence that it has been carefully considered and evaluated.

It's important to know that the idea of *patience* (and strategic *waiting*) goes against the common trend of the day that focuses on instant gratification and moving fast. Moreover, this trend is usually associated with a rather low level of tolerance when things don't go according to our expectations and as quickly as we thought they should. This impatience can compromise not only potential opportunities but important relationships as well. It's also important to note that there is only so much we can do in controlling what happens in life, and after we have done everything possible, we must wait without forcing the results. Patience is often viewed by some as a weakness or being too passive. However, this view is missing the point of what we are trying to convey here. Patience isn't a blind resignation to destiny ("What will happen will happen") — it is temporarily suspending or delaying our decisions so that we can more fully gather critical information and plan our actions accordingly. Generally, once we have taken the time to understand situations, we also gain understanding of how long we should wait or delay action on matters. Although we may think that we know what's necessary to achieve our goals, we may not know how long it will take to accomplish those goals.

On how best to improve patience, some of the oldest thinking on the subject has been that we first must acquire *knowledge*. The thinking is that we will develop an expertise in a particular area (or areas), discover that our knowledge is finite or limited, and learn what we need to know about setting goals and the time it takes to accomplish these goals. Amongst other things, this will teach us to live with a certain amount of uncertainty regarding the extent to which we are able to control things. When we learn how much is in our control and how much is not, it becomes easier to determine when we've done all we can do.

Threats Associated with Very Low Levels of Impulse Control:

Impulsiveness makes it difficult for us to act in a controlled fashion and frequently leads to self-defeating behavior. The threat of significant weaknesses in this area is the classic failing to "think before you act scenario," leaving us dependent upon gut instincts, which is located too far away from the real seat of wisdom. Acting impulsively can cost us dearly in many ways, whether it be because of the missteps that we make on the job or personally having impulsive spending habits, being hot tempered, or having difficulty controlling the use of alcohol. On an organizational level, the threat often equates to costly rework and wastage as well as lost opportunities; repeated mistakes of this nature can be catastrophic for the corporation and threaten its very existence.

Bottom Line Suggestions for Improving Impulse Control

"Personal Remedies":

- Think about how it feels when you are about to lose control, and how you feel when you lose control. Write those feelings down.
- Ask yourself how it affects you and others when you lose control. Put that down in writing, and think about it from time to time.
- Make a list of situations and people that play a part in your losing control, and try to understand what really happens and why.
- In a constructive manner, try to deal with those situations that make you angry. If you can't eliminate these sources of deep anger and frustration, try to avoid them as much as possible.
- Make an effort to relax more and not to get upset about unimportant things. Be less emotional about things in general.
- Be more patient with others. Make a habit of listening more and talking less.
- Don't interrupt others — let them finish what they have to say before responding.
- Speak slower and softer.
- Avoid conflicts with others and getting dragged into confrontations.
- The next time you feel like you're going to lose control, try not to think about what is upsetting you at the moment; just leave it, disengage, and do a 180-degree on the spot. Do something else like getting some fresh air, going for a walk, or doing some other form of physical exercise or work while clearing your head and focusing on nothing.

"Group Remedies":

- Be aware of potentially explosive situations at work, and try to defuse and neutralize them.
- Try not to team up employees who have impulse control problems with others at work who tend to aggravate them.
- Encourage impulsive people to take things a bit easier at work, to wind down, not to get too excited about things or to make a big thing

over nothing.

- Encourage impulsive and impatient employees to verbalize what bothers them rather than keeping it in.
- If you see an explosion coming on, tell the person to disengage, to back away, to leave the room, take a walk, and return later after things have calmed down.
- Organize a group at work, or perhaps a retreat, in which you discuss impulse control and how to improve it.
- Explain what is impulse control and why it's important for one's overall ability to successfully cope with daily demands.
- Emphasize why improving this skill will have an overall positive effect on the productivity of the organization as a whole.
- Run through some basic stress reduction strategies, and discuss a few tactics for controlling anger.
- Encourage them to discuss what typically creates an explosive situation for them and how they can better control it.
- Have them talk about the consequences of their impulsive behavior. Then encourage constructive feedback related to steps that can be taken to curb this type of behavior.

PART 5:
General Mood

General mood consists of two basic factors: *optimism* and *happiness*. This area taps one's general attitude and outlook on life as well as one's ability to enjoy life and overall feeling of contentment. When this area is elevated, it typically indicates optimistic, positive, hopeful, and cheerful individuals who know how to enjoy life. In addition to being an essential element in interacting with others, this general area plays a motivational role in problem solving and stress tolerance. Individuals who possess enhanced general mood help create an uplifting and positive atmosphere in the workplace. Our research findings have demonstrated that successful marketing and PR consultants have significantly high levels of general mood.

Optimism

Optimism is the ability to look at the brighter side of life and to maintain a positive attitude even in the face of adversity. Optimism assumes a measure of hope in one's approach to life. It is a positive approach to daily living. Optimism is the opposite of pessimism, which is a common symptom of depression. There is a strong connection between one's degree of optimism and one's ability to cope with problems.

Optimism plays an important role in overall self-motivation and is a very important factor in reaching goals and coping with stress; all of this is important for managerial competencies.

Strengths Associated with High Levels of Optimism:

People with high levels of optimism are able to look at the brighter side of life and maintain a positive attitude, even in the face of adversity. These individuals typically feel sure of themselves in most situations, believe they can stay on top of tough situations, hope for the best, and are generally motivated to continue even when things get difficult. They usually expect things will turn out right in the end, believe in their ability to handle most upsetting problems, and typically don't feel they will fail when they begin something new. Optimists experience many of the same life events as pessimists, but the difference is that optimists weather these situations better and bounce back quicker from defeat by learning from their mistakes, while pessimists typically give up easier. Strength in this area is critical to success in sales and marketing based on our research. Other studies have also shown that optimists do significantly better in these occupations than those who are less optimistic. The idea is that optimism lies in what we tell ourselves — I think, therefore I am. Individuals who possess high levels of optimism have drive and motivation that acts like an internal engine helping them persevere despite setbacks and eventually succeed...because they fully expect to. This is, essentially, the idea of the self-fulfilling prophecy. Although we can choose to see the negative aspects and tell ourselves why we can't do it, optimists approach the same issues differently. They tend to see a difficult situation as a *challenge* that they want to tackle and overcome, while pessimists see it as a mountain too high to climb — so why bother? It's what we choose to tell ourselves or latch on to about a situation. Optimists choose to latch on to the positive — they see the negative, but tend to put it into a different perspective. Pessimists tend to find the most negative scenario and the worst possible outcomes and then latch onto them, ignoring and dismissing other ways of looking at it.

From an organizational perspective, to be high in optimism is like having an additional power source that drives employees to strive, overcome, and succeed. A famous line from an old Clint Eastwood movie illustrates the essence of optimism. Clint played the Marine Gunnery

Sergeant Tom Highway in the movie *Heartbreak Ridge*. "Gunny" Highway was trying to shape up a platoon of irreverent misfits. He continually challenged them by doing the unexpected. When they complained and felt like throwing in the towel, he quipped, "Improvise, adapt, and overcome." This is an excellent example of what optimists routinely do. Situations aren't always the best, so they improvise…they make do with what they have without giving up, in quest of their goal. Second, they adapt to the situation…they bloom wherever they are planted. Pessimists tend to complain about the situation and place…"If I was only working in a better office, I could do better." Contrary to this approach, the optimist says: "These might not be optimal conditions, but I can make do…adapt to these surroundings and still do my job." Third, optimists typically persist until they overcome. It's all about *not quitting*. A classic trait exhibited by Marine Gunnery Sergeant Tom Highway was the ability to know how far to push his people, not allowing them to quit. In the end, they realized that they had gone further than they ever thought they could, which in turn raised their level of self-confidence and expectancy; they learned the value of self-discipline and not allowing yourself to quit.

Weaknesses Associated with Low Levels of Optimism:

Weakness in this area implies difficulty with one's general outlook and view of the world. Our beliefs become the rose-colored glasses through which we view our world, interpret and assign meaning to events, and determine our corresponding course of action. Weakness in this area equates to pessimism, which is like a computer software virus — infecting and corrupting both the interpretation and processing of the input the computer receives as well as the readability of its output. Pessimism affects what we see, how we interpret it, and the meaning we assign to it, which in turn has an ill effect on our actions. If you have ever tried to interact with a virus-infected computer, you will recall how unpleasant that experience was for you (the end-user). Interacting with pessimistic individuals and organizations is also an unpleasant experience, particularly for optimistic people.

Having a pessimistic attitude is like having cataracts — it clouds our vision and perception affecting the way we navigate through life.

Additionally, this makes establishing meaningful interpersonal relation-ships difficult at work as well as in one's private life. As we move into the era of intellectual capital where team-based interaction, collaborative communities of practice, corporate ecosystems, and social forms of learning will be important, weaknesses in this area will not contribute to effective interaction and performance. The premium will be placed on a certain degree of optimism necessary to deal with incessant change, uncertainty, and entrepreneurial risk. Optimism will be requisite to persevere and flourish in this new environment.

Potential Opportunities Associated with Average Levels of Optimism:

One possible way of improving optimism was related by the hero from *Heartbreak Ridge*. The Gunnery Sergeant Tom Highway model for increasing optimism is as follows:

(1) **Improvise:** Optimism is boosted by one's sense of confidence expectancy. Confidence expectancy is gained through receiving training, education, and knowledge that contribute to one's belief that he or she can handle the situation at hand whatever it might be. This includes the ability to operate in both favorable and unfavorable conditions as well as to bounce back from setbacks and failures. Confidence expectancy is gained through spending the time required to gain a sense of mastery in the tools one must use, which is oneself (one's self) in the era of the knowledge worker. Once we have developed a sufficient level of confidence expectancy, we are more able to improvise with an optimistic calm and with the belief that we can overcome. There are a number of stories of airline pilots whose confidence expectancy in themselves and in their professional skills allowed them to recover from serious equipment failure and land their aircraft safely preventing untold loss of life. Their ability to "make do" (to improvise) was often key to their success. Their level of optimism was based on and related to their confidence expectancy and training in dealing with suboptimal conditions in order to overcome serious mechanical malfunctions. To do so, they were taught to think critically from a systems perspective, allowing them to improvise when a system

or component of a system fails to function optimally. It is the same in other aspects of life. If we can only deal with the optimal, we will be in for a rough ride. Once we've trained to overcome failure perhaps equally as well, we have begun to pave the way for the confidence expectancy that is foundational for optimism and the belief that we can handle difficult situations.

(2) **Adapt:** To adapt means to acclimate, accommodate, adjust, conform, fit, reconcile, square with, and so on. The idea is to adjust to a given situation, survive, and continue to evolve with it. This is frequently seen in nature as it relates to the survival of certain species, which hinges on their ability to adapt and evolve. The bottom line is that belief in one's resiliency and ability to adapt enhances optimism, which allows one to successfully accommodate most situations — "I can do it…I'll do it…I did it." Adapting follows improvising — "I did it, because I knew how to do it." An example of this is that of an airline pilot who lost control of his ailerons (that part of the plane that helps the aircraft turn). In order to continue to navigate towards the runway, he was able to improvise upon discovering that he could steer with the plane's rudder. He then adapted by transferring to rudder-based steering. After he noticed that the aircraft took longer to turn and couldn't turn as sharply, he once again improvised and adapted his turning techniques to factor this in. In this example, improvising meant determining a way to fly with what the pilot had to work with — the rudder. The pilot then adapted to this improvised reality of flight with no ailerons and to all the changes that he needed to factor in to survive in the post-aileron environment. In this example and in countless other examples in the real world, we often have to ask ourselves how do we adapt in order to continue to function after we have to improvise. Whereas improvising is determining ways to compensate for some change, adapting is modifying our behavior to accommodate for these changes.

(3) **Overcome:** The last part of this approach to increase optimism is to overcome. The idea is that if we have improvised because of some change and adapted to accommodate for it, we then have to see it through until we overcome the problem that was created by the change. Once the above-mentioned pilot improvised a way to

steer without the ailerons and adapted to a post-ailerons existence, he then saw it through to the landing, thus overcoming the situation. This, in essence, is persistence in the face of adversity. However, the problem with many of us is that we quit prematurely, and by doing this, we fail to learn what we could have learned by overcoming a problem and thereby gaining the optimism and confidence expectancy involved in going through this process.

Threats Associated with Very Low Levels of Optimism:

The threat stemming from significant deficits in optimism is obvious. From an individual perspective, being pessimistic can have an ill effect on our ability to deal with challenges because we are too pessimistic to try or because we give up too quickly. Additionally, behaving in such a manner tends to prevent us from establishing and maintaining meaningful mutually beneficial relationships with others — few people enjoy being around pessimistic people. Organizationally, a spirit of pessimism can corrupt the organizational culture and create difficulties in retaining personnel, in maintaining long-term relationships with customers, and in strategically planning for the future.

The story of Scrooge is a good example of the ultimate threat associated from being overly pessimistic. According to the story, Scrooge lost the joy of life and deteriorated to a dismal existence. This is, in essence, is the real threat of pessimism — becoming thoroughly corrupted by the virus of negativism.

Bottom Line Suggestions for Improving Optimism

"Personal Remedies":

- See what feels better and why: being pessimistic or being optimistic.
- How does it affect you and others when you are pessimistic.
- Make more of an effort to look at the brighter side of life.

- Try not being so serious about things in general.
- Make a list of positive affirmations and review them from time to time.
- Try being more hopeful when dealing with problems and difficult situations.
- Make an effort to maintain a more positive attitude, even when the going gets tough.
- Be alert to pessimistic thoughts that you may have, and look at them more objectively and less emotionally. Even try a 180-degree tactic — turn pessimistic thoughts into positive ones.
- Purposely suppress pessimistic thoughts when they arise.
- Experiment with adopting a more positive outlook about things in general.

"Group Remedies":

- Try to create a more positive and optimistic atmosphere at work.
- Set an example for others by being more optimistic and hopeful.
- Make an effort to be more positive about things around others.
- Discourage pessimistic people from working together — try placing them with more optimistic employees if possible.
- Try to deploy optimistic people in key positions at work.
- Convey that you're optimistic and hopeful that the group will accomplish its goals successfully, and encourage others to feel the same.
- Encourage others to give more positive feedback.
- Give constructive and supportive feedback when goals are not successfully met, and convey the feeling of hopefulness that the situation will be rectified in the future.
- Organize a group at work, or perhaps a retreat, in which you can discuss optimism and how to improve it.
- Explain what is *optimism* and why it's important for coping effectively with daily demands at work and elsewhere.
- Emphasize why improving this skill will have an overall positive effect on the productivity of the organization as a whole.

Happiness

Happiness is the ability to enjoy oneself and others, to feel satisfied with one's life, and to have fun. Happiness combines self-satisfaction and general contentment with the ability to enjoy life. This component of emotional, personal, and social intelligence involves the ability to enjoy various aspects of one's life and life in general. Happy people often feel good and at ease both at home and at work, they are able to "let their hair down" and enjoy opportunities for having fun. Happiness is also associated with a general feeling of cheerfulness and enthusiasm. This is also an important by-product and barometric indicator of one's overall degree of emotional and social intelligence and functioning. At the opposite end of this factor is *sadness*, which can turn into actual *depression* if it is severe enough or lasts for a long time. These people typically tend to worry, feel uncertain about the future, and lack energy and drive to do things; in more severe cases, they tend to feel chronically guilty and dissatisfied with their lives, withdraw socially, and even entertain suicidal thoughts at times.

Strengths Associated with High Levels of Happiness:

Individuals who are able to feel satisfied with their lives, genuinely enjoy the company of others, and have the ability to derive pleasure from life possess high levels of happiness; these people commonly have a happy disposition and are pleasant to be with. It's fairly easy for them to smile and laugh, and they are typically cheerful and like to have fun. They have little difficulty enjoying life and are not overly obsessed with work — they enjoy their leisure time. Generally, strength in this area indicates good emotional and social functioning.

Based on a ten-year study of happiness, David Myers and Ed Diener provide an excellent summary of some of the more significant research findings related to this factor (*Scientific American*, May 1996). They indicate that happy people are less self-focused, less hostile and abusive, and are less susceptible to disease than others. They found that age is not a good predictor of happiness, nor is gender, race, or economic status. Strength in this area has been associated with high performance on the job, particularly in those occupations that frequently interact with customers such as sales and marketing. Additionally, happiness has shown to be very important in building high performance work groups and teams — others seem to enjoy being in the presence of happy people who are seen as easy to get along with. The degree to which one fits in with and likes their coworkers is closely related to retention, especially in today's hot job market. Organizationally, strength in this area relates to higher performance and the ability to avoid the devastating effects that a negative emotional virus can foster.

Weaknesses Associated with Low Levels of Happiness:

As was previously mentioned, weaknesses in this area are typically manifested by feelings of sadness, a tendency to worry, feeling uncertain about the future, and a general lack energy and drive to do things. Within organizations, these individuals are often seen as negative *naysayers* and *spoilers*, and others frequently do not like to be around them and may even seek to actively avoid them. If the entire organization is low in happiness, it is evidence of an emotional-social virus that can have a devastating effect on the entire work system from interpersonal relations, group cohesion, general stress level, retention and turnover, and customer relations to overall productivity. Since this factor also acts as a barometer for overall emotional and social functioning, low levels of happiness are symptomatic of problems in other areas.

In dealing with low levels of individual and organizational happiness, the most effective leverage is gained by seeking out root causes rather than merely treating the symptoms. For example, when individuals are unhappy, we are often tempted to give them time off or move them to another area in an effort to "fix" these symptoms. A higher leverage approach is to explore the drivers of this behavior. It could be that the individual lacks the skills necessary to progress, feels a sense of being trapped or hopeless, or might be experiencing difficulty in interpersonal relations on the job and thereby feels isolated from the group. The idea here is to seek and address the root cause, instead of just the medicating the symptoms. It is logical to assume that in most instances of significant weaknesses in this area, the individual is most likely experiencing skill deficits in other areas as well that impact happiness. In some individuals, a general depressive and pessimistic style has become their way of relating to the world, and they seem to be determined to see things no other way. These people may feel that others tend to avoid them and may consciously or unconsciously act in a manner that ensures that this will happen. When this inevitably does happen, it becomes a self-reinforcing feedback loop (the *self-fulfilling prophecy*); quite often, they conclude that "I knew they didn't like me," which only serves to perpetuate this behavior. Organizationally, these feedback loops can perpetuate a negative organizational culture over long periods of time and force new hires to either adopt this prevailing virus or leave.

Potential Opportunities Associated with Average Levels of Happiness:

In an effort to explore various ways of improving happiness, it's important to return to the above-mentioned research conducted by Myer and Diener (*Scientific American*, May 1996). They identified four basic traits of happy people that were consistently noted in their study:

1. They like and accept themselves, especially in the more individual-istic western cultures. This translates to positive self-esteem and a belief and confidence in oneself.
2. They typically feel in control of their lives. On the other hand, it was found that those with little or no control over their lives tend to experience impaired mood and poor health.
3. They are usually optimistic.
4. They are typically extroverted and are happy whether alone or with others.

Furthermore, the positive relationships that happy people typically have with others are also directly correlated with better physical health and longer life. Their research findings also revealed that married people tend to be happier than people who are not married. In another survey conducted by the National Opinion Research Center in the 1970s and the 1980s, 39 percent of married adults reported that they were "very happy" compared to 24 percent of those who were never married and to 12 percent of those who were divorced. In the same survey, religious people reported a greater feeling of happiness than less religious people. Another survey found that very religious people to be twice as likely as those who said that they were less religious to describe themselves as "very happy." In another study of 166,000 people in fourteen countries, self-perceived happiness and satisfaction with life were found to be positively correlated with the frequency of attendance at religious services. With respect to these findings, some researchers think that this is due to greater social support and feelings of hopefulness that are thought to be part of religious affiliation.

One way to improve happiness begins with first examining our attitude towards failure. We are less likely to react to defeat with feelings of sadness if we are able to acknowledge that we failed at something rather than seeing ourselves as a failure. Failure should be constructively turned around and experienced as a stepping stone on the path to success rather than as a personal defeat. The idea is to cultivate an optimistic attitude towards doing better next time, the belief that you can overcome or change the current setback and that such setbacks are temporary. Happiness and optimism are fairly complementary, highly correlated, and tend to enhance one another. Additionally, there is some evidence that being able to forgive and to ask forgiveness can increase one's ability to feel happy and be more productive. Focusing more on positive and productive thoughts and actions has also found to be helpful. What's frequently lacking to transform failures into success is perseverance and courage. Perseverance helps us remain faithful to our goals and face obstacles and discouragement along the way. Without some degree of perseverance and tenacity, we would not be able to fully experience the happiness that accompanies accomplishing our goals and making an honest effort to actualize our potential. Abraham Lincoln's life provides a good example of this type of tenacity in the face of setbacks:

- He suffered the death of both his mother and his sister when he was very young.
- He suffered the death of two of his young sons.
- He suffered from depression in his early thirties.
- He failed as a businessman.
- He was defeated when he ran for Senator in 1855 and in 1859.
- He was defeated for the nomination of vice president in 1856.

Yet in spite of all of these setbacks in his private and public life, he was elected President of the United States and is remembered more for his successes than for his personal defeats and failures.

Another way to enhance happiness is to have a sense of *purpose* that makes us feel that we are living a meaningful life. For example, doing volunteer work and something to help others gives us a good feeling. Happiness seems to be more a function of internal than external factors, often resulting from a feeling that we are living a good and meaningful life — a life with a purpose and worth living.

As was previously mentioned, exercise and relaxation techniques have a positive effect on mood. One should consider such activity as an adjunct to maintaining positive mood.

The saying that "laughter is the best medicine" suggests that we might also consider the benefits of this very simple and human behavior for increasing a sense of happiness. At the least, it is a very natural way of rapidly relaxing tense muscles and creating an immediate feeling or surge of well-being. Laughter is also thought to have a positive effect on our ability to fight illness as is suggested in Norman Cousins' book titled *Anatomy of an Illness*; he described how he would watch videotaped comedies to facilitate laughter. We also need to make and take the time for pleasurable activities. It has been shown that when we work on things that we enjoy doing, the blood chemistry is altered in such a way that it increases the body's resistance to disease and infection.

Lastly, it's important to note that, organizationally, a powerful tactic to deal with pessimistic attitudes is to act in a manner inconsistent with what is expected — like returning kindness for hurt.

Threats Associated with Very Low Levels of Happiness:

As was previously mentioned, the major threat associated with significantly low levels of happiness is a predisposition towards depression. Since happiness serves as a barometric indicator of one's overall degree of emotional and social intelligence and functioning, extremely low levels of this factor indicate that things are currently not going that well on many fronts. More precisely, it indicates the presence of an *emotional-social virus* that is currently having an ill effect on the way we relate to ourselves, the manner in which we relate to others, our ability to deal with problematic situations and change, our ability to handle stress, and our overall motivational level. Organizationally, this situation is caustic and can have a devastating effect on the entire system, especially if the executive leaders are contaminated with the same disease. This organizational disease is typically manifested by attitudes of defeat and despair, which not only corrupts the organizational culture, but harms the company's bottom line as well.

In the era of intellectual capital, we are fooling ourselves to think that people will voluntarily share their creativity and entrepreneurial spirit with us when they feel they are working in an unhealthy and dangerous environment. It is important to reiterate that the workforce attitude, more than aptitude, will determine its altitude in the end.

Bottom Line Suggestions for Improving Happiness

"Personal Remedies":

- Make a list of things that make you happy and things that make you sad, and try to understand why.
- How does it affect you and others when you're sad?
- If you can't eliminate the things that make you sad, try to avoid those people and situations that have a bad effect on you.
- Complain less, think positive, and try to enjoy life more.
- Do more things that make you feel good, and spend more time with people who like having fun and enjoy life; try to work with happy people — it rubs off.
- Look at having fun as a valuable goal in and of itself and as an important part of your life.
- Think what you like doing for entertainment, and set aside more time for activities that make you feel good. Then simply go ahead and do more of those things.
- Learn to enjoy humor and to tell a good joke from time to time — but laugh *with* people and not at them.

- See a good comedy from time to time, and really get into it.
- Try to cheer up people when they are sad (try to get a laugh out of them) — it will make you feel good as well, and if that doesn't work, avoid them!

"Group Remedies":

- Try to promote a positive and uplifting atmosphere at work. For example, provide small awards and have special lunches to celebrate good team performance. Make coming to work a pleasant experience and a nice place to be — get the work done, but have a nice time while you're at it!
- Celebrate the completion of a project with some sort of social activity.
- Think about "casual days" at the end of the week and month, or a (non-alcoholic) "happy hour" at work from time to time.
- Seize the opportunities for social get-togethers at work and outside of the workplace.
- Organize group vacations and trips that include the employees' significant others.
- Discourage depressive behavior or reactions at work. Your aim should be to work on establishing and maintaining a positive, optimistic, and pleasant corporate culture.
- Make an effort to place the more depressive employees with more jovial ones.
- Organize a group at work, or perhaps a retreat, in which you discuss happiness and how to improve it.
- Explain what is meant by *happiness* and why it's important for one's overall ability to successfully cope with daily demands.
- Emphasize why improving this skill will have an overall positive effect on the productivity of the organization as a whole.
- Explain the positive effect of happiness on others and on the general atmosphere at work.

Epilogue

The purpose of this book was to expose the reader to a breakthrough method of improving organizational effectiveness and productivity. The secret to accomplishing this bottom line of every organization is to know how to find, hire, train, promote, and retain people with the "right stuff" through *human capital profiling*. It was also stressed that the people skills that routinely characterize those with the right stuff are skills associated with emotional and social intelligence — one of the biggest factors that leverages the success of individuals and organizations. These are identified and measured by doing an *emotional and social audit* of the organization's most valuable asset — its employees. This approach has vital implications for the survival and future success of companies. It provides the map and compass required to navigate in the era of the knowledge worker. This is what will be required to develop the kind of employees, managers, and executive leaders of tomorrow's corporate world.

Afterword

"where the rubber meets the road"

We have reviewed a great deal of material in the preparation of this book, but have decided to share only the more relevant research findings and ideas for fear of overwhelming the reader. To receive additional suggestions for improving the various emotional and social skills that were discussed, the reader is referred to the Appendix below, which lists a number of self-help books. Those who are interested in high-performance solutions for optimizing individual and organizational performance are invited to visit **http://www.equniversity.com.** "EQ University" was founded to "Optimize People" through the online BarOn EQ-i assessment, web-based training courses matching each of the fifteen areas assessed by the BarOn EQ-i, as well as individual coaching.

Appendix: Self-Help Books (and Audio/ Visual Tapes)

APPENDIX A: *Where to Find More Ideas for Improving Self-Regard*

Aldrige, J. *Self Esteem*, 1995

Anderson, W. *The Confidence Course*, 1997

Beattie, M. *Stop Being Mean to Yourself*, 1997

Branden, N. *Achieving High Self Esteem*, 1997 (audio/visual tape)

Branden, N. *The Six Pillars of Self Esteem*, 1995

Cleghorn, P. *The Secrets of Self Esteem*, 1996

Field, L. *The Self Esteem Workbook*, 1995

Field, L. *60 Tips for Self Esteem*, 1997

Gray, J. *Raising Your Self Esteem*, 1996 (audio/visual tape)

Linderfield, G. *Self Esteem*, 1997 (audio/visual tape)

Markham, U. *Creating a Positive Self Image*, 1995

APPENDIX B: *Where to Find More Ideas for Improving Emotional Self-Awareness*

Branden, N. *The Art of Living Consciously*, 1997

Burley-Allen, M. *Listening: The Forgotten Skill*, 1995

McKay, M. *Messages*, 1995

APPENDIX C: *Where to Find More Ideas for Improving Assertiveness*

Anderson, W. *The Confidence Course*, 1997
Bruno, F.J. *Little Keys Conquer Shyness*, 1997
Canfield, J. *The Aladdin Factor*, 1995
Elgin, S. *Disagree Without Being Disagreeable*, 1997
Lindenfield, G. *Assert Yourself*, 1997 (book and audio/visual tape)
McKay, M. *Messages*, 1995
Schneier, F. *Hidden Faces of Shyness*, 1996

APPENDIX D: *Where to Find More Ideas for Improving Independence*

Branden, N. *Taking Responsibility*, 1997
Cameron, B. *The Artist's Way*, 1995

APPENDIX E: *Where to Find More Ideas for Improving Self-Actualization*

Anderson G. *Living Life on Purpose*, 1997
Andreas, S. *NLP – The New Technology of Achievement*, 1996
Bennett, V. *I've Found the Keys, Now Where's the Car*, 1996
Brown, L. *It's Not Over Until You Win*, 1998
Choquette, S. *Your Heart's Desire*, 1997
Dyer, W. *Four Pathways to Success*, 1997 (audio/visual tape)
Graham, S. *You Can Make It Happen*, 1997
Katselas, M. *Dreams into Action*, 1996
Keyes, K. *Your Road Map to Lifelong Happiness*, 1995
Rowe, D. *Successful Self*, 1996
Sharma, R.S. *The Monk Who Sold His Ferrari*, 1997

APPENDIX F: *Where to Find More Ideas for Improving Empathy*

Burley-Allen, M. *Listening: The Forgotten Skill*, 1995
Cameron, J. *The Artist's Way*, 1995
Coit, L. *Listening*, 1996
Covey, S. *Seven Habits of Highly Effective People*, 1989 (book & audio/visual tape)
McKay, S. *Listening*, 1995 (audio/visual tape)

APPENDIX G: *Where to Find More Ideas for Improving Social Responsibility*

Branden, N. *Taking Responsibility*, 1997
Covey, S. *Seven Habits of Highly Effective People*, 1989 (book & audio/visual tape)

APPENDIX H: *Where to Find More Ideas for Improving Interpersonal Relationship*

Covey, S. *Seven Habits of Highly Effective People*, 1989 (book & audio/visual tape)
Martinet, J. *The Art of Mingling*, 1996 (audio/visual tape)
McKay, M. *Messages*, 1995

APPENDIX I: *Where to Find More Ideas for Improving Reality Testing*

Butler, G. *Managing Your Mind*, 1997
Ellis, A. *A New Guide To Rational Living*, 1975

APPENDIX J: *Where to Find More Ideas for Improving Flexibility*

Mallinger, A. *Too Perfect*, 1991

APPENDIX K: *Where to Find More Ideas for Improving Problem Solving*

Butler, G. *Managing Your Mind*, 1997
DeBono, E. *Teach Yourself to Think*, 1997 (audio/visual tape)
Ellis, A. *A New Guide To Rational Living*, 1975
Gelb, M. *Creative Genius*, 1997 (audio/visual tape)
Hart, A. *Habits of the Mind*, 1996
Lorayne, H. *Secrets of Mind Power*, 1996
Siler, T. *Think Like a Genius*, 1997

APPENDIX L: *Where to Find More Ideas for Improving Stress Tolerance*

Ali, M. *What Do Lions Know about Stress*, 1997
Babior, S. *Overcoming Panic, Anxiety and Phobias*, 1995
Bassett, L. *From Panic to Power*, 1997
Bourne, E.J. *The Anxiety and Phobia Workbook*, 1995 (book & audio/visual tape)
Bruno, F.J. *Little Keys to Stop Worrying*, 1997
Fensterheim, H. *Conquer Your Phobias and Anxieties*, 1996
Fensterheim, H. *Relieve Stress in 10 Days*, 1996 (audio/visual tape)
Gray, J. *Releasing Fear and Anxiety*, 1996 (audio/visual tape)
Lawson, M. *Facing Anxiety and Stress*, 1996
Reiner, R. *Manage Stress*, 1997 (audio/visual tape)

APPENDIX M: *Where to Find More Ideas for Improving Impulse Control*

Dentemaro, K. *Straight Talk About Anger*, 1996
Ellis, T. *Control Your Anger Before It Controls You*, 1997 (audio/visual tape)
Livingstone, S. *Dealing with Your Anger*, 1997

APPENDIX O: *Where to Find More Ideas for Improving Optimism*

Bennett, V. *I've Found the Keys, Now Where's the Car*, 1996
Peale, N. *Amazing Results from Positive Thinking*, 1996
Peale, N. *Toughminded Optimist*, 1996
Peale, N. *The Power of Positive Thinking*, 1996 (book & audio/visual tape)

APPENDIX P: *Where to Find More Ideas for Improving Happiness*

Bennett, V. *I've Found the Keys, Now Where's the Car*, 1996
Brami, E. *Little Moments of Happiness*, 1997
Carlson, R. *You Can Be Happy No Matter What*, 1997
Cohen, A. *Joy Is My Compass*, 1996
Keyes, K. *Your Road Map to Lifelong Happiness*, 1995
Resnick, S. *The Pleasure Zone*, 1997

References

1. Bar-On, R. (1988). The development of a concept of psychological well-being. Unpublished doctoral dissertation, Rhodes University, South Africa.

2. Bar-On, R. (1992). The development of a concept and test of emotional intelligence. Unpublished manuscript.

3. Bar-On, R. (1996a). The Bar-On Emotional Quotient Inventory (EQ-i): A test of emotional intelligence. Toronto, Canada: Multi-Health Systems

4. Bar-On, R. (1996b). The era of the EQ: Defining and assessing emotional intelligence. Poster session presented at the 104th Annual Convention of the American Psychological Association, Toronto, Canada.

5. Bar-On, R. (1996c). A cross-cultural study of emotional intelligence. Paper presented at the 83rd Indian Science Congress, Patiala, India.

6. Bar-On, R., Dupertuis, D. G., & Garrido, M. A (1996). Cross-cultural and cross-gender study of psychological well-being using the EQ-i. Symposium conducted at the 13th Congress of the International Association for Cross-Cultural Psychology, Montreal, Canada.

7. Bar-On, R. (1997a). Bar-On Emotional Quotient Inventory: Technical Manual. Toronto, Canada: Multi-Health Systems.

8. Bar-On, R. (1997b). Bar-On Emotional Quotient Inventory: User's Manual. Toronto, Canada: Multi-Health Systems.

9. Bar-On, R. (1997c). Bar-On Emotional Quotient Inventory: Facilitator's Resource Manual. Toronto, Canada: Multi-Health Systems.

10. Bar-On, R. (1997d). The development of the Bar-On EQ-i: A measure of emotional intelligence. Poster session presented at the 105th Annual Convention of the American Psychological Association, Chicago, Illinois.

11. Bar-On, R. (1998a). Development of a Model and Measure of Noncognitive Intelligence (Emotional, Personal and Social Intelligence). In print.

12. Bennis, W. (1997). Organizing Genius: The Secrets of Creative

Collaboration. Reading, MA.:Addison-Wesley.

13. Benson, H. (1975). The Relaxation Response. New York: Morrow

14. Benson, H. (1993). The Wellness Book: The Comprehensive Guide To Maintaining Health and Treating Stress-Related Illness. New York: Simon & Schuster.

15. Berlew & Hall (1966). The Socialization of Managers: Effects and Expectations Upon Performance. Administrative Science Quarterly.

16. Branden, N. (1995). Six Pillars of Self Esteem. New York: Bantam Books.

17. Cantor, N., & Kihlstrom, J. (1987). Social intelligence: the cognitive basis of personality. In P. Shaver (Ed.), Review of Personality and Social psychology (Vol. 6, pp. 15–34). Beverly Hills, CA: Sage.

18. Collins, J. (1997). Built To Last: Successful Habits of Visionary Companies. New York: Harper Business.

19. Corts, D., & Gowing, M. (1992). Dimensions of effective behavior: Executives, managers, and supervisors. PRD-92-05. Washington, DC: U.S. Office of Personnel Management.

20. Cousins, N. (1979). Anatomy Of An Illness. New York: Norton.

21. Covey, S. (1989). The Seven Habits Of Highly Effective People. Thorndike, ME: G. K. Hall.

22. Doll, E. (1935). A genetic scale of social maturity. American Journal of Orthopsychiatry, 5, 180–188.

23. Doll, E. (1953). The measurement of social competence. Minneapolis: American Guidance Service.

24. Drucker, P. (1995). Managing In A Time Of Great Change. New York: Penguin Books.

25. Dubrin, A. (1997). Magnetism: Discover Your Own Charisma And Learn To Charm, Inspire And Influence Others. New York: Amacom Books.

26. Dunkley, J. (1996). The psychological well-being of coronary heart disease patients before and after an intervention program. Unpublished master's thesis, University of Pretoria, South Africa.

27. Dupertuis, D. (1996). The EQ-i and MMPI-2 profiles of a clinical sample in Argentina. Unpublished manuscript.

28. Dupertuis, D., & Bar-On, R. (1996a). A comparative study of Argentinean and American populations with the MMPI-2 and EQ-i.

Paper presented at the MMPI Conference, Minneapolis, Minnesota.

29. Dupertuis, D., & Bar-On, R. (1996b). Culture, personality, and psychological well-being. Paper presented at the 8th Argentine Congress of Psychology, San Luis, Argentina.

30. Dupertuis, D., & Bar-On, R. (1996c). A comparative study of Argentinean and American populations with the MMPI-2 and EQ-i. Paper presented at the Annual MMPI Conference, Minneapolis, Minnesota.

31. Eliot, R. (1995). From Stress To Strength. New York: Bantam.

32. Ellis, A. (1975). A New Guide To Rational Living. Edgewood Cliffs: NJ: Prentice-Hall.

33. Ellis, J. (1997). American Sphinx: The Character Of Thomas Jefferson. New York: Alfred Knopf.

34. Englebart, D. (1996). Boosting Collective IQ: A Design For Dramatic Improvements in Productivity, Effectiveness, and Competitiveness. Fremont, CA: Bootstrap Institute.

35. Eyde, L., & Schay, B. (1997). Managerial competencies: Foundation for cost effective selection. A paper presented in a symposium on Managerial Competencies: Between g and Hard Data at the 12th Annual Conference of the Society for Industrial and Organizational Psychology, St. Louis, Missouri.

36. Fensterheim, H., & Baer, J. (1975). Don't say yes when you want to say no. New York: David McKay.

37. Fisher, R. (1996). Beyond Machiavelli: Tools For Coping With Conflict. New York: Penguin.

38. Flesch, R. (1948). A new readability yardstick. Journal of Applied Psychology, 32, 221–233.

39. Flett, M. (1996). The psychological well-being of the alcoholic: Evaluation of a treatment program. Unpublished master's thesis, University of Pretoria, South Africa.

40. Frankl, V. (1995). Man's Search For Meaning. New York: Pocket Books.

41. Galassi, M., & Galassi, J. (1977). Assert Yourself! How To Be Your Own Person. New York: Human Sciences Press.

42. Gardner, H. (1983). Frames of Mind. New York: Basic Books.

43. Gardner, H. (1993). Multiple Intelligences: The Theory and Practice. New York: Basic Books.
44. Gardner, J. (1983). Self-Renewal: The Individual And The Innovative Society. New York: Norton.
45. Garrido, M. (1996). Acculturation and emotional well-being among Latinos in Rhode Island. Paper presented at the 13th Congress of the International Association for Cross-Cultural Psychology, Montreal, Canada.
46. Goleman, D. (1995). Emotional Intelligence. New York: Bantam Books.
47. Goodland, J. (1984). A Place Called School. New York: McGraw-Hill.
48. Gregory, D., & Park, R. (1992). Occupational study of federal executives, managers, and supervisors: An application of the Multipurpose Occupational Systems Analysis Inventory – Closed Ended (MOSIAC). PRD-92-21. Washington, DC: US Office of Personnel Management.
49. Grove, A. (1997). Only The Paranoid Survive: How To Exploit The Crisis Points That Challenge Every Company and Career. New York: Doubleday.
50. Handley, R. (1997). AFRS rates emotional intelligence. Air Force Recruiter News.
51. Hansen, M. & Canfield, J. (1993). Chicken Soup For The Soul. Deerfield Beach, FL: Health Communications.
52. Hansen, M. & Canfield, J. (1995). A Second Helping Of Chicken Soup For The Soul. Deerfield Beach, FL: Health Communications.
53. Hee-Woo, J. (1998). Emotional Intelligence and Cognitive Ability as Predictors of Job Performance in the Banking Sector. Unpublished MA dissertation, Ateneo de Manila University, Philippines.
54. Herzberg, F. (1968). One More Time: How Do You Motivate Employees? Harvard Business Review.
55. James, G. (1996) Business Wisdom Of The Electronic Elite. New York: Random House.
56. Jones, L. (1995). Jesus, CEO: Using Ancient Wisdom For Visionary Leadership. New York: Hyperion.
57. Jones, L. (1996). The Path: Creating Your Personal Mission

Statement For Work And Life. New York: Hyperion.

58. Kaplan, H., & Sadock, B. (1991). Comprehensive Glossary of Psychiatry. Baltimore, MD: Williams & Wilkins.

59. Kelly, G. (1955). The Psychology Of Personal Constructs. New York: Norton.

60. King, L. (1995). How To Talk To Anyone, Anytime, Anywhere: The Secrets Of Good Conversation. New York: Crown Trade Paperbacks.

61. Kirkcaldy, B. (1995). The Kirkcaldy Quality of Life Questionnaire. An unpublished test.

62. Leeper, R. (1948). A motivational theory of emotions to replace "emotions as disorganized responses." Psychological Review, 55, 5–21.

63. Levine, M. (1996). Take It From Me: Practical And Inspiring Career Advice From The Celebrated And Successful. New York: Berkeley Publishing Group.

64. Livingston, J. (1988). Pygmalion in Management. Harvard Business Review.

65. Loren, M. (1996). The Road To Virtue: Resolutions For Daily Living Inspired By The Wisdom of Ben Franklin. New York: Avon Books.

66. MacLean, P. (1949). Psychosomatic disease and the 'visceral brain': Recent developments bearing on the Papez theory of emotion. Psychosomatic Medicine, 11, 338–353.

67. Maslow, A. (1954). Motivation & Personality. New York: Harper.

68. Mayer, J., DiPalo, M., & Salovey, P. (1990). Perceiving affective content in ambiguous visual stimuli: A component of emotional intelligence. Journal of Personality Assessment, 54 (3–4), 772–781.

69. Mayer, J., Mamberg, M., & Volanth, A. (1988). Cognitive domains of the mood system. Journal of Personality, 56, 453–486.

70. Mayer, J., & Salovey, P. (1993). The intelligence of emotional intelligence. Intelligence, 17 (4), 433–442.

71. Mayer, J., & Salovey, P. (1995). Emotional intelligence and the construction and regulation of feelings. Applied and Preventive Psychology, 4 (3), 197–208.

72. Mayer, J., & Salovey, P. (1997). What is Emotional Intelligence? In P. Salovey & D. Sluyter (Eds.), Emotional Development and Emotional Intelligence: Implications for Educators. New York: Basic Books.

73. Mayer, J., Salovey, P. Gomberg-Kaufman, S., & Blainey, K. (1991). A

broader conception of mood experience. Journal of Personality and Social Psychology, 60, 100–111.

74. Miller, J. (1996) Best Boss/Worst Boss. Arlington, TX: Summit Publishing Group.

75. Moss, F., Hunt, T., Omwake, K., & Woodward, L. (1949). Social intelligence test, George Washington University Series. Washington, DC: Center for Psychology Service.

76. Myers, D. & Diener, E. (1996). The Pursuit Of Happiness. Scientific American, May.

77. O'Grady, S. (1995). Return With Honor. New York: Doubleday.

78. Pallazza, R., & Bar-On, R. (1995). A study of the emotional intelligence of convicted criminals. Unpublished manuscript.

79. Patino, R. (1997). Success Is A Choice: Ten Steps To Overachieving in Business And Life. New York: Broadway Books.

80. Peterson, C., Semmel, A., von Baeyer, C., Abramson, L., Metalsky, G., & Seligman, M. (1982). The Attributional Style Questionnaire. Cognitive Therapy and Research, 16, 287–300.

81. Robbins, A. (1991). Awaken The Giant Within. New York: Simon & Schuster.

82. Robbins, A & Mclendon, J. (1997). Unlimited Power: A Black Choice. New York: Simon & Schuster.

83. Rosenthal, R. & Jacobsen, L. (1968). Pygmalion In The Classroom. New York: Holt, Rhinehart, & Winston.

84. Ruesch, J. (1948). The infantile personality. Psychosomatic Medicine, 10, 134–144.

85. Scott, G. (1990). Resolving Conflict: With Others and Within Yourself. Oakland, CA: New Harbinger.

86. Salovey, P., & Birnbaum, D. (1989). Influence of mood on health-relevant cognitions. Journal of Personality and Social Psychology, 57, 539–551.

87. Salovey, P., Hsee, C., & Mayer, J. (1993). Emotional intelligence and the self-regulation of affect. In D. M. Wegner and J. W. Pennebaker (Eds.), Handbook of Mental Control (pp. 258–277). Englewood Cliffs, NJ: Prentice-Hall.

88. Salovey, P., & Mayer, J. (1989–90). Emotional intelligence. Imagination, Cognition and Personality, 9 (3), 185–211.

89. Salovey, P., Mayer, J., Goldman, S., Turvey, C., & Palfai, T. (1985). Emotional attention, clarity, and repair: Exploring emotional intelligence using the Trait Meta Mood Scale. In J. Pennebaker (Ed.). Emotion, Disclosure, & Health (pp. 125–154). New York: Bantam Books.

90. Salovey, P., Mayer, J., & Rosenhan, D. (1991). Mood and helping: Mood as a motivator of helping and helping as a regulator of mood. In M. S. Clark (Ed.), Prosocial behavior: Review of Personality and Social Psychology, Vol. 12 (pp. 215–237). Newbury Park, CA: Sage.

91. Scott, G. (1990). Resolving Conflict: With Others and Within Yourself. Oakland, CA: New Harbinger

92. Seligman, M., Abramson, L., Semmel, A., & von Baeyer, C. (1979). Depressive attributional style. Journal of Abnormal Psychology, 88, 242–247.

93. Shevetz, Y., Stir, S., & Bar-On, R. (1996). The EQ-i profiles of in-patients suffering from mood disorders and schizophrenia. Unpublished manuscript.

94. Siegel, B. (1986). Love, Medicine, and Miracles: Lessons Learned About Self-Healing From A Surgeon's Experience With Exceptional Patients. New York: Harper Collins.

95. Sifneos, P. (1967). Clinical observations on some patients suffering from a variety of psychosomatic diseases. Acta Medicina Psychosomatica, 7, 1–10.

96. Sifneos, P. (1973). The prevalence of 'alexithymia' characteristics in psychosomatic patients. Psychotherapy and Psychosomatics, 22, 255–262.

97. Spearman, C. (1927). The Abilities of Man. New York: The Macmillan Co.

98. Spitzer, Q. & Evans, R. (1997). Heads You Win: How The Best Companies Think. New York: Simon & Schuster.

99. Sternberg, R. (1996). Successful Intelligence:How Practical And Creative Intelligence Determines Success In Life. New York: Simon & Schuster.

100. Sternberg, R. (1997). The concept of intelligence and its role in lifelong learning and success. American Psychologist, 52 (10), 1030–1037.

101. Stewart, T. (1997). Intellectual Capital. New York: Doubleday.

102. Swart, A. (1996). The relationship between well-being and academic performance. Unpublished master's thesis, University of Pretoria, South Africa.

103. Taylor, G., Bagby, R., & Parker, J. (1997). Disorders of affect regulation: Alexithymia in Medical and Psychiatric Illness. Cambridge, England: Cambridge University Press.

104. Thorndike, R., & Stein, S. (1937). An evaluation of the attempts to measure social intelligence. Psychological Bulletin, 34, 275–84.

105. Wagner, R. (1997). Intelligence, Training, and Employment. American Psychologist, 52 (10), 1059–1069.

106. Wechsler, D. (1940). Nonintellective factors in general intelligence. Psychological Bulletin, 37, 444–445.

107. Wechsler, D. (1943). Nonintellective factors in general intelligence. Journal of Abnormal Social Psychology, 38, 100–104.

108. Wechsler, D. (1958). The measurement and appraisal of adult intelligence, 4th edition. Baltimore, MD: The Williams & Wilkins Company.

109. Yandrick, R. (1996). Behavioral Risk Management. San Francisco: Jossey-Bass.